Megalithomania

JOHN MICHELL

Megalithomania

*Artists, antiquarians and archaeologists
at the old stone monuments*

with 220 illustrations, 8 in color

Cornell University Press

ITHACA, NEW YORK

Half-title page: Some of the old stone monuments and curiosities figured in early antiquarian books. From Cambry's *Monumens celtiques*, 1805.

Title page: Investigations at Carnac by French savants at the beginning of the nineteenth century.

Contents page: Images of 'celtomania' in Brittany, 1845.

© 1982 Thames and Hudson Ltd, London

All rights reserved. Except for brief quotations in a review, this book, or parts thereof, must not be reproduced in any form without permission in writing from the publisher. For information address Cornell University Press, 124 Roberts Place, Ithaca, New York 14850.

Published 1982 by Cornell University Press.

International Standard Book Number: 0-8014-1479-2

Library of Congress Catalog Card Number: 81-69643

Color reproduction by Cliché Lux, La Chaux-de-Fonds, Switzerland.
Black and white reproduction by D.S. Colour London.
Typeset, printed and bound by Everbest Printing Co. Ltd., Hong Kong.

Contents

The problem in archaeology is when to stop laughing

Dr Glyn Daniel
Antiquity December 1961

1 Megalithomania

Up to a few years ago, most of the thousands of megalithic sites throughout Western Europe were little visited other than by professional archaeologists, whose one, primitive method of investigation, with spade and pickaxe, has added considerably to the damage still being done by farmers, builders, foresters, roadmakers and anyone else who covets their sites or materials. A vast tonnage of ancient treasures had been dug out from the monuments where they were carefully placed four or more thousand years ago, often to be lost or destroyed or, at best, to be reburied in the vaults of museums. In the process of yielding up their spoils, a great many prehistoric monuments have been damaged or totally obliterated, leaving a sadly reduced stock of antiquities for scientific study in the present and future. And the most damning criticism of excavations at ancient sites, whether by simple treasure-hunters or highly trained archaeologists, is that the sum total of all their labours has contributed scarcely at all to resolving the problem obviously presented by the substantial presence of megalithic monuments, the problem of why they were built.

That problem is now being attacked by other methods than excavation, and by professors of other disciplines than archaeology. The first outsiders to enter the field of megalithic studies were the astronomers. Ever since the eighteenth century it has been widely suggested that Stonehenge and other stone circles were in some way related to the heavenly bodies. At first the idea was supported by little more than Caesar's report on the astronomical knowledge and cosmology of the Celtic Druids, to whom these monuments were then attributed. Such classical references to Druid learning, and the evidence in ancient Irish and Welsh texts of an astronomical science among the early Celts, were generally dismissed as being irrelevant to the study of megalithic monuments after these had been shown to predate by many centuries the first appearance of the Celts in Britain. Yet by the end of the nineteenth century several studies of ancient sites had been published, notably by Sir J. Norman Lockyer in *The Dawn of Astronomy*, 1894, on the orientations of Egyptian temples, and by him and Mr A.L. Lewis in articles on stone circles in Britain, demonstrating that all these monuments had been erected by people with a keen interest in astronomy. In the early years of this century the astronomical interpreters of prehistoric sites flourished, and attracted followers in Ireland and Brittany. All sorts of people joined in, from professional surveyors to clergymen and mystics, creating a wave of popular enthusiasm for megalithic sites or, as here styled, 'megalithomania'.

The outbreak of megalithomania, inspired by Lockyer and stimulated in 1909 by the publication of the complete edition of his *Stonehenge and Other British Monuments Astronomically Considered*, was eventually quelled by the archaeologists. A brief account of their battle with the astronomers, in which the latter were for a time routed from the megalithic field, is given in a previous book by the writer of this one, *A Little History of Astro-archaeology*. More recent surges of megalithomania have featured other approaches than the astronomical. In the 1920s and 1930s a club formed by readers of Alfred Watkins's *The Old Straight Track*, 1925, was active around megalithic monuments, investigating the phenomenon of aligned sites or 'leys' which Watkins had first noticed in Herefordshire. This movement also was heavily discouraged by the archaeologists who, by the end of the Second World War, had reasserted their exclusive right to megalithic sites and their interpretation.

It was not until the middle of the 1960s that the belief in excavation as the sole or primary useful method of antiquarian research was again challenged by astronomers, this time far more formidably than in the days of Lockyer, with proofs and arguments firmly based on statistics; and the retired professor of engineering, Alexander Thom, whose book, *Megalithic Sites in Britain*, 1967, caused the greatest disturbance to established patterns of archaeological thought, not only showed that megalithic sites were everywhere related to each other as centres or markers for astronomical observation, but revealed the stone circle builders as adepts of geometry and number in the Pythagorean tradition.

Thom's conclusions gave new heart to admirers of *The Old Straight Track*, who identified his long-distance, astronomically directed sighting lines between megalithic sites with the straight lines between monuments which Watkins had called 'leys'. Their long-lapsed journal, *The Ley Hunter*, resumed publication and acted as host to the wide range of new theories and observations of antiquity which symptomized the revived megalithomania of the late 1960s onward. This time it afflicted not only astronomers but geometers, dowsers, mathematicians, occultists, spiritual revivalists, UFOlogists and other students of modern folklore, and also certain electronics experts who, at the time of writing, are engaged in a prolonged exercise of measuring the seasonal intensity of electro-magnetic energies in the neighbourhood of the Rollright stone circle in Oxfordshire.

The more the merrier perhaps. The megalith problem is a complicated one with many different aspects, and it is appropriate therefore that researchers with different types of knowledge and insight should be engaged in solving it. And at least the astronomers, dowsers and other non-archaeologists now infesting prehistoric sites do them no damage, and by widening popular interest in them contribute towards their preservation.

All this excitement about a collection of battered old rocks and mounds of earth must seem puzzling to those who have yet had no direct experience of

Caractacus, in his retreat among the Welsh Druids, receives some British soldiers: an episode from William Mason's influential poem, *Caractacus*, illustrated in 1799. In the background is the Druid apparatus of mistletoe-hung oak, stone altar, stone circle and hermits' cells. On the right, monkish figures, or possibly early ley hunters, proceed down a sacred avenue towards a distant rocking stone.

megalithomania. To them especially this book is dedicated, with the author's kindly-intended wish that it may help to infect them. To that end, the appeal of megalithomania is here illustrated in two ways, first by showing some of the sites and monuments that give rise to it, as depicted over the years by antiquarian artists, draughtsmen and photographers, and secondly by summarizing the many different sorts of theories and ideas that people have derived from them. Megalithic studies have been distinguished by remarkable feats of scholarly imagination, quite as picturesque in their effects as anything produced by the artists; and the reason why so many learned or perceptive people have found the subject attractive is that it touches on such fundamental matters as the origins of human culture and the first principles behind the development of modern civilization and science. The monuments themselves, and the ways in which they relate to their natural surroundings, give evidence that their creators combined many different skills and types of knowledge to achieve the purpose for which the great stones were designed. That purpose is still unknown, but it is not beyond inquiry, and the problem is sufficiently deep and subtle to be worthy of anyone's attention.

William Stukeley at Grantham, 1726.

2 The megalithic revivalism of Dr Stukeley

The first explosion of megalithomania was set off by a Lincolnshire doctor turned clergyman, William Stukeley (1687–1765). The genius of this man has never been justly acknowledged. It was a peculiarly English genius. Like William Cobbett a century later, and with a similar gift for discerning layers of history behind the contemporary appearance of the countryside, Stukeley rode through most of the English counties making notes of everything that interested him. Sometimes he travelled alone, sometimes with convivial parties of fellow antiquarians, members of the Society of Roman Knights which he had formed among his friends for the purpose of recording and preserving Roman remains in Britain. It was unique in its time in admitting women members. Each of the Knights took a Celtic or Roman name, Stukeley's being Chyndonax the Arch-Druid.

The first book of Stukeley's antiquarian tours, *Itinerarium Curiosum*, published in 1725, was a fine folio volume wonderfully illustrated with his engraved drawings. As records of ancient monuments these have never been surpassed. Archaeologists still refer to Stukeley's plates and to the volumes of his manuscript notes and sketches, many of them now in the Bodleian Library at Oxford, as accurate accounts, often the only ones ever made, of monuments now vanished. The most delightful feature of his drawings is that they show the ancient sites in relation to their local countryside, providing glimpses of old England before the great changes which were wrought by the enclosures of its commons. His topographical eye was later to perceive sacred symbols laid out over large areas of landscape by the ancient Druids, but throughout his earlier career Stukeley had no particular notion of Druids. His drawings were made direct from nature, unconditioned by his own or other people's theories, and his notes were factual records of such monuments as came to his notice.

As he approached the age of forty a change came over Dr Stukeley. For some years he had been living in London as secretary of the newly founded Society of Antiquaries, enjoying the company of scholars among whom he was recognized as the first authority on British ancient monuments. In 1726 he suddenly moved away from London and took a house in Grantham. The following year he married, and the year after that he became a clergyman of the Church of England. Behind these moves was evidently some kind of revelation or born-again conversion which altered the direction of his career. From a gregarious young scholar Stukeley became a man with a mission – or, in the words of his contemporaries, 'fanciful'.

A decade earlier, after seeing David Loggan's engraving of bustards flying over Stonehenge, he had been attracted by that monument, and even more so by the neighbouring temple at Avebury. He had spent several seasons at both places, surveying and drawing, providing a unique record of parts of the Stonehenge avenue since obliterated and of stones at Avebury which, even as he was drawing them, were being broken up by men like farmer Robinson whose cruel features are preserved in Stukeley's portrait. In the seventeenth century, John Aubrey had identified Stonehenge and Avebury as temples of the Druids. This Stukeley accepted, and the more he studied the works of the old British priests, the more impressed he became by their wisdom and learning. Aspects of the Druid science, never dreamed of by earlier scholars, were revealed to him, such as the use by the Stonehenge builders of the magnetic compass. The inspirational atmosphere of ancient sites began to affect him. Of Stonehenge he noted that 'it pleases like a magical spell', and he grew to realize that the Druids had 'advanced their inquiries, under all disadvantages, to such heights as should make our moderns ashamed, to wink in the sunshine of

Stukeley's recognition of earthworks in various parts of Britain as alate, or winged, temples coincided with the development of his belief that the winged disc was an ancient image of Deity. In this sketch of 1759 one of his winged temples in a grove is the scene of 'The Midsummer Sacrifice of the Druids'.

Another of Stukeley's reconstructions of ancient festivals. His 'Druid-sacrifice of the Vernal Equinox' illustrates some effects of his attempted reconciliation of Druidism with the Church of England.

The Midsummer Sacrifice of the Druids.

Stukeley delin. 1759.

The Druid-sacrifice of the vernal Equinox.

Stukeley delin. 1759.

learning and religion'. It was not merely the arts and skills of these people that he learnt to admire, but the sublime nature of their philosophy. Suddenly he was seized by an idea, so grand and noble that it affected his entire cast of mind, the idea that the Druids had first proclaimed in Britain the very same principles of true, patriarchal religion as were now upheld by the Church of England. Were this information to be published, its effect would be to rout the deists, freethinkers and opponents of Christianity through irrefutable proofs of their error, and to reconcile all other religions, including the Jewish, with the true English Church, leading eventually to 'what many learned men have thought; that here was to be open'd the glory of Christ's kingdom on earth'.

Directly from this realization followed Stukeley's retirement to Grantham, his marriage, his entry into the Church and his undertaking of a many-volumed work on Patriarchal Christianity. In it he was to trace the history of the world from its creation, describing the origins of true religion and idolatry, the persistence of the former in the teachings of Moses, Plato and the post-Reformation English Church, and its appearance in Britain with the coming of the Phoenicians together with the Druids. The solid ground behind all this was to be the evidence provided by Stonehenge and Avebury. The historical part of the work was never accomplished, but the two volumes which appeared, *Stonehenge, a Temple Restored to the British Druids*, in 1740 and *Abury, a Temple of the British Druids*, three years later, summarized Stukeley's theories to the astonishment of his contemporaries.

The prime exhibit in Stukeley's demonstration that 'the true religion has chiefly, since the repeopling mankind after the flood, subsisted in our islands' was his survey of Avebury. The famous plate in his book shows its stone circles and avenues forming over several miles of country the image of a serpent passing through a ring. A circle formerly standing on the ridge called Hackpen Hill made up its head, which Stukeley in his published plan slyly 'improved' into an oval. Hackpen, he declared, meant Serpent's Head, and the entire Avebury image was an ancient, universal symbol of the deity in accordance with Christian orthodoxy, the great circle representing the Father or First Cause, from which proceeded the Saviour in the traditional form of a serpent. This was the 'noble monument of our ancestors' piety, I may add, orthodoxy' with which Stukeley proposed to reconvert the world to the true patriarchal religion and to bring about the New Jerusalem in Britain.

Although there is yet no obvious sign of Stukeley's grand object being achieved, his Druid propaganda has proved highly effective. Reconstituted in 1781 by one Henry Hurle in accordance with Stukeley's ideas, the 'Ancient Order of Druids' has flourished ever since, and their right to occupy Stonehenge at the summer solstice, despite attempts by historical purists to oust them, is now established as it were from time immemorial. In reaction to this, and with the turn of fashion against speculative antiquarianism, Stukeley's reputation among archaeologists was for many years lowly rated. Yet his later works were not primarily addressed to scholars. With *Abury* he was not, as he put it, 'pretending to a formal and stiff scholastic proof of every thing I say, which would be odious and irksome to the reader, as well as myself'. His appeal was to his readers' imagination, and his intent was to whip up their enthusiasm for megalithic sites in England, thus exposing themselves to the influence of true, native, Druid religion. For a similar purpose, to attract divine influences, the great serpent temple at Avebury had, as Stukeley perceived the matter, originally been designed:

'And it was the way of the ancients in their religious buildings, to copy out

The Druid-sacrifice of Yule-tide.

Stukeley delin. 1759.

Stukeley's 'Druid-sacrifice of Yule-tide'. A glimpse of the prehistoric Wiltshire landscape, with Silbury Hill, the infant river Kennet and the serpent temple of Avebury in the background.

or analogize the form of the divine being, as they conceiv'd it, in a symbolic manner. By this means they produc'd a most effectual prophylast, as they thought, which could not fail of drawing down the blessings of divine providence upon that place and country, as it were, by sympathy and similitude.'

Popular enthusiasm was indeed whipped up by Stukeley's antiquarian works, and when, a few years before his death, the heroic verses of Ossian, a prehistoric bard from the Scottish islands, were first made public, evidently supporting many of the claims Stukeley had made for the high culture of the Celtic Druids, enthusiasm boiled over into 'celtomania'. About his own work Stukeley had written that 'the curious will find sufficient room to extend it'; and so they did. For over a hundred years people continued to hunt out Druidical 'dracontia' or serpent temples, which Stukeley had classified thus: simple rings as at Rollright (Rholdrwyg or Druid's wheel as Stukeley derived it); serpents made up of stone avenues or alignments; and serpent figures with wings.

The majority of antiquarians in and after Stukeley's time had little sympathy for the dracontium notion. Dr William Borlase drily observed from Cornwall that he had seen many of the circular type of Druid temple but never any of the serpent variety. Yet there has always been an undercurrent of support for Stukeley's dracontia, occasionally breaking into the open, as when General Maudet de Penhouët, aided and abetted by the English serpent-seeking archaeologist, the Rev. J. Bathurst Deane, identified Carnac as a French rival to the dracontium at Avebury. And at about the same time, towards the middle of the nineteenth century, an undisputable dracontium,

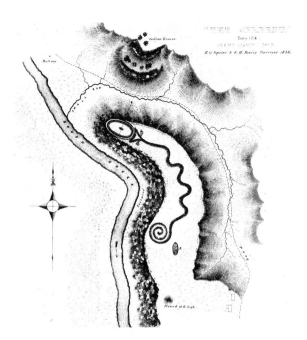

The great serpent mound of Adams County, Ohio, engraved in 1846. The discovery of this 1254-feet-long earthen serpent, apparently in the act of swallowing an egg, heartened Stukeley's remaining followers in the nineteenth century and encouraged new searches for serpent temples in Europe. Modern explainers have interpreted the Ohio serpent mound as an astronomical symbol. People have also reported terrifying or visionary experiences at the site.

the Great Serpent Mound of Ohio, was discovered in America. Stukeley has been much abused for slightly fudging one of his Avebury plates so as to make his serpent more realistic, but modern archaeology has shown that the original Avebury groundplan was probably much as he drew it; and the serpent formed by its avenues does indeed resemble the universal sign of the mercurial streams of vital currents within the earth's surface which modern dowsers have found to be associated with the sites of ancient sanctuaries. An item of folklore which would have delighted Stukeley was recorded in 1909 by Lord Avebury in his introduction to R. Hippesley Cox's *Guide to Avebury:* that the area round the stones was locally regarded as so sacred that no snakes could live there, and if any were introduced they would immediately die.

The greatest extension of Stukeley's work has been made by poets, notably by the man who became his prophet, William Blake. The noble, generous vision behind Stukeley's account of Avebury and Stonehenge deeply affected Blake, who captured it and gave it sublime expression in his final prophecy, *Jerusalem*. Stukeley had hoped that the Jews, whom he regarded as being more at home in England than in any other country of the world, would be early converts to his C-of-E Druidism, thus legitimizing his proposed New Jerusalem in Britain. Inspired with the notion, and repeating several of Stukeley's phrases, Blake hurled the following exhortation at the Jews in the introduction to the second chapter of his work, vehemently reminding them of their Druidic inheritance:

'Jerusalem the Emanation of the Giant Albion! Can it be? Is it a Truth that the Learned have explored? Was Britain the Primitive Seat of the Patriarchal Religion? If it is true, my title-page is also True, that Jerusalem was & is the emanation of the Giant Albion ...

'All things Begin and End in Albion's Ancient Druid Rocky Shore.

'Your Ancestors derived their origin from Abraham, Heber, Shem and Noah, who were Druids: as the Druid Temples (which are the Patriarchal Pillars & Oak Groves) over the whole Earth witness to this day.'

Blake further illustrates his debt to Stukeley in his drawing of the Avebury dracontium together with elements of Stonehenge, representing with this image the science of prehistoric Britain as discerned by his antiquarian predecessor. He was not, however, the Druidolater that Stukeley had been. He must have known an earlier book, *Britannia Antiqua Illustrata*, a learned history of archaic Britain by Aylett Sammes, published in 1676. In it Sammes describes the primeval reign of the Bardic order in Britain. The Bards were Phoenician giants whose customs were founded on eternal poetic truths, inspirationally received and enunciated in the Orphean manner. They were replaced by a later wave of Phoenician immigration which brought in the Druids, and these priestly bureaucrats formalized the Bardic customs into rigid laws which they enforced by cruel punishments including (on the authority of Caesar) burning criminals alive in great wickerwork effigies. They offered sacrifices to their gods, instead of music as the Bards had done, although their laws were on the whole just and highly principled. Blake as a natural Bard differed therefore from Stukeley who was an antiquarian, a clergyman, a friend of Newton and a natural Druid. They agreed with each other that Stonehenge and Avebury were temples of the Druid religion once spread out over the earth, embracing both the English and the Jews, but whereas Stukeley took the serpent at Avebury as a symbol of the true universal religion, to Blake it was 'Mystery, Babylon the Great, the Druid dragon and hidden Harlot'.

Jerusalem, with the 'Patriarchal Pillars & Oak Groves' of the original Druids, whom Sammes would have called the Bards, was corrupted during the sleep of their parent, Albion, and the iron rule of the latter-day priests created Babylon, where

> *The Serpent Temples thro' the Earth, from the wide Plain of Salisbury,*
> *Resound with the cries of Victims, shouts and songs and dying groans.*

The differences between Blake and Stukeley are those between poet and priest. Blake's golden age was a state of inspired anarchy while Stukeley's was one of sacred order. Politically therefore they were at odds, but as prophets they were united by their common vision of the New Jerusalem on earth, first to be revealed in England. Together they ensured that megalithic studies would never in future be entirely secular, and that Stonehenge and Avebury would be as much the rightful property of artists and mystics as of archaeologists.

As a tailpiece to his *Abury* (1743), Stukeley made a portrait of Fierce Farmer Robinson, the churlish 'stone-killer' who used fire and water to break up many of the Avebury stones. The lugubrious background includes a stone being cracked over a burning pit.

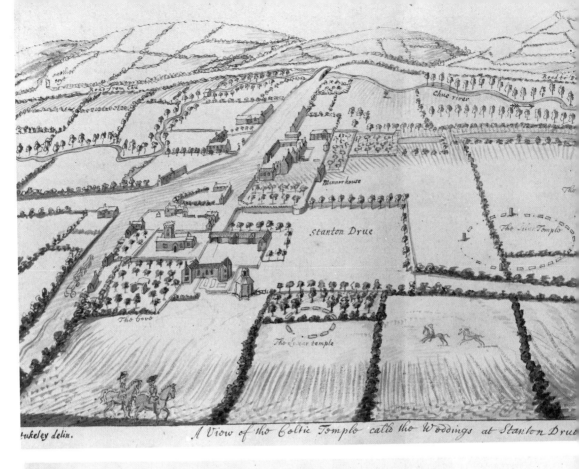

Stukeley delin.

Manner house

Stanton Drue

Chue river

The Elder Temple

The Lesser temple

The Cove

A View of the Celtic Temple call'd the Weddings at Stanton Drue

A Prospect of Abury from the South side of the Val
19 July 1723.

make this plate a little longer at both ends

Some examples of William Stukeley's curious imagination and of his genius as a topographical draughtsman.

Above: The hermitage of a Druid priest, Chyndonax's cell in the Grove of Hébé, drawn by Stukeley in 1748. The idea for this inspired reconstruction came from a rustic dwelling in Wales, sketched during one of his tours.

Left: The wonderful view of the stone circles and surrounding landscape of Stanton Drew in Somerset, drawn by Stukeley in July 1723. The circles here, as in Stukeley's early drawings of Avebury, are interpreted astronomically. In the middle distance is the outlying stone, Hautville's Quoit, and another is shown, top left, which no longer exists. On the horizon are the ramparts of Maes Knoll, an ancient enclosure on the line of the Wansdyke.

Below, left: Stukeley's 'Prospect of Abury from the South Side of the Vallum', drawn in the same month as the Stanton Drew scene *above.* An appended note instructs the engraver to 'bring that house (marked A) a little lower down'.

Below: 'The great Temple & Grove of the Druids at Trerdrew in Anglesea', a mysterious megalithic composition recorded by Stukeley in this drawing which was engraved to illustrate his *Itinerarium Curiosum* of 1725.

The great Temple & Grove of the Druids at Trerdrew in Anglesea . p. 19.

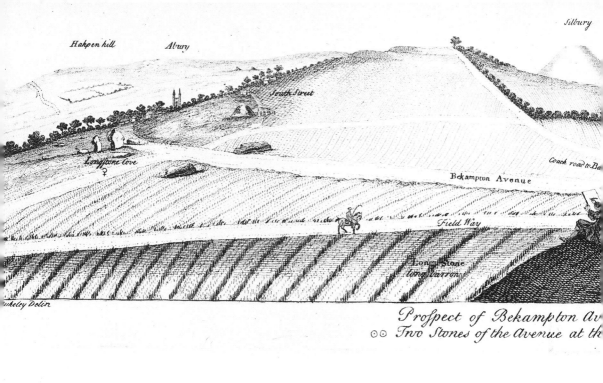

Hakpen hill   Abury   Silbury

South Street

Longstone Cove

Coach road to Ba

Bekampton Avenue

Field Way

Long Stone
long barrow

Stukeley Delin

Prospect of Bekampton Av
oo *Two Stones of the Avenue at th*

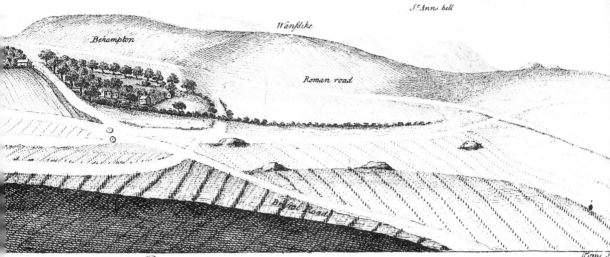

Bristol Road

Tom J.

...om Longston long Barrow 1724
...ing of the two Roads demolish'd by R.^d Fowler. B. the Termination of the avenue.

Three of the illustrations to Stukeley's *Stonehenge* and *Abury*, part of his great achievement in recording details of the monuments (as in his drawing of a Stonehenge trilithon, *opposite*) and, at the same time, showing how they stand in relation to other neighbouring landmarks. A fine example is his 'Prospect of Beckhampton Avenue' (*above*), drawn in 1724. All the remaining stones in the avenue, which formed the tail of the Avebury stone serpent, have long since vanished. In his 'View of the Kist-Vaen in Clatford bottom' (*below*), as in many of his illustrations, Stukeley includes the figures of himself and party sketching and investigating the monument, an agreeable habit which was later taken up by other antiquarian artists. In the stone-littered valley below the stone now commonly called The Devil's Den, near Avebury, the antiquarians' carriage awaits the resumption of their tour.

View of the Kist-Vaen in Clatford bottom.

On his Kentish tour of 1722 Stukeley made several drawings of the monument called Kit's Coty House, near Aylesford (*above*), which, like the nearby ruined Lower Coty House or Countless Stones (*below*), was identified variously in local legend as a memorial to a British or Saxon king killed in a battle between the two in AD 455 or as a relic of ancient sorcery. The low earthwork labelled The Grave in the upper picture is supposed by some authorities, against the opinions of others, to be the remains of a mound which once covered the stone monument. Scarcely a trace is now to be seen of the great stone rows which were recorded up to the nineteenth century in the vicinity of the Coty House.

Opposite: Three examples of Stukeley's skill in discerning and depicting the ancient features of a landscape. From his *Itinerarium Curiosum:* the line of Ermin Street through Ancaster in Lincolnshire; the Devil's Arrows at Boroughbridge, Yorkshire; South Cadbury, the Camelot of Arthurian legend, in Somerset, with a glimpse in the foreground of the open fields cultivated in the local manner.

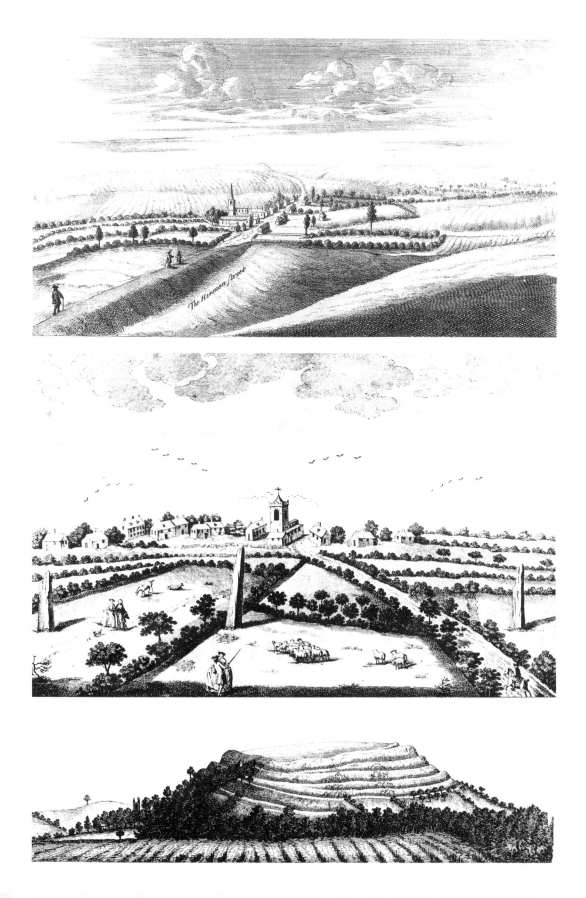

The Hermen street

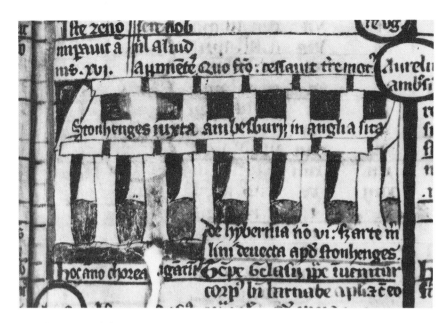

Stonhenges iuxta Amberbury in anglia sita

de hybernia no vi: & arte in
lim deuecta apo ftonhenges

3   Views of Stonehenge

This, the earliest
known image of
Stonehenge, from a
fourteenth-century
manuscript, is unique
in making it rectan-
gular.

The earliest legends of Stonehenge, as recorded by medieval chroniclers,
made it the scene of a battle or massacre. Later antiquarians supposed it to
have been the scene of priestly sacrifices. No proof of these theories has ever
been discovered and they have long dropped out of fashion. But even if they
have no relevance to anything that happened at Stonehenge in the past, they
were certainly true in relation to its future. For Stonehenge is now acknowledged as the classic battleground of archaeology, where scholarly reputations
are sacrificed and where every new generation massacres the theories of its
predecessors.

When was it built? and why? and who did it? The vast literature on Stonehenge offers the widest conceivable range of answers, or guesses. Various authors have attributed it to the Phoenicians, Romans, Danes, Saxons, Celtic
Druids, British aborigines, Brahmins, Egyptians, Chaldeans, and even (in
W.S. Blacket's *The Lost Histories of America*, 1833) the Red Indians. Giants,
dwarfs and supernatural forces were suggested by several of the pre-scientific
writers. The post-scientific ones have added Atlanteans and extra-terrestrials.
It has been called a temple, an observatory, a memorial, a parliament, a
necropolis, an orrery, a stone-age computer, and much besides. One might
almost suppose that it was specially designed to accommodate every notion
that could possibly be projected onto it. For at Stonehenge no antiquarian
cause is ever finally lost – as witnessed by the curious history of the Stonehenge Druids.

John Aubrey in the seventeenth century was the first author to record his
opinion, in his long unpublished manuscript, *Monumenta Britannica*, that
Stonehenge was a temple 'of the Priests of the most eminent Order, viz,
Druids'. Yet even this may not have been the first attribution to the Druids,
for at the beginning of his *Stone-Heng Restored*, published posthumously in
1655, Inigo Jones (1573-1652) went to great lengths, as if to refute an opposing
school of thought, to show that Stonehenge could *not* have been built by the

ancient Britons or their Druid rulers. His reasons were that the Druids, although skilful in astronomy and philosophy, were not recorded as having any knowledge of architecture. They did not build temples, but held rites in natural groves. When he began his Stonehenge work, Inigo Jones had just returned from Rome, and he recognized the British monument as an expression of the classical architectural principles as given by Vitruvius. It was, he decided, an example of the Tuscan order, built soon after the Roman invasion.

Inigo Jones's Roman attribution came under heavy attack from other Stonehenge authorities, and though stoutly defended by his friend, John Webb (*A Vindication of 'Stone-Heng Restored'*, 1665), the Roman cause went into decline. Aubrey accused Inigo Jones of sharp practice in that he 'framed the monument to his own hypothesis, which is much differing from the thing itself'. Aubrey's own Stonehenge plan was a great improvement on Inigo Jones's classicized version, and his Druid theory was widely favoured by the scholarly until, by the middle of the eighteenth century, following the publication of Stukeley's *Stonehenge* and *Abury*, it had become almost universally accepted.

The identification of Stonehenge as a temple of the Druids paved the way for a further theory which, more frequently than all others, has recurred throughout the modern history of the monument: the theory that Stonehenge was designed in relation to the heavens as a temple-observatory where prehistoric astronomers could watch and record the movements of the sun and moon. This could be justified in two ways. First, Caesar and other classical writers state that the Druids practised astronomy in connection with their philosophy and divination; secondly, the axis of Stonehenge, together with the avenue leading up to it, is orientated towards the point of sunrise at midsummer. This feature had been remarked by Stukeley in 1740, and in 1770 Dr John Smith published his *Choir-Gaur*, the first astronomical interpretation of Stonehenge as a Druid temple, 'erected in the earliest years for observing the motions of the heavenly bodies'.

From Smith's time, and throughout much of the nineteenth century, the most commonly expressed theory about Stonehenge identified it as a solar or astronomical temple of the Druids. This theory, however, took many different forms, and there were many who dissented from it. For lack of historical or scientific means of dating the monument, there was no way of proving its Druid origin, and a reaction against that theory, and against the idealized Druid image as presented by Stukeley, gained powerful adherents. As late as 1872 James Fergusson in his account of megalithic structures throughout the world, *Rude Stone Monuments*, revived the tradition, first set down by Geoffrey of Monmouth in the twelfth century, that Stonehenge was a monument to the British nobles treacherously murdered by the Saxons in about AD 462; that its stones had originally been brought from Ireland; and that it was the sepulchre of Aurelius Ambrosius. The most cantankerous of Stonehenge literary warriors, Fergusson poured scorn on Druids and ancient astronomers, as well as on every writer past or present who had suggested a pre-Roman date for Stonehenge. On Stukeley's works he was particularly hard: 'Had so silly a fabrication been put forward in the present day [1872], it would probably have met with the contempt it deserves.' In this style Fergusson exemplified the ill-tempered, invective-as-argument habit which has disfigured so much modern archaeological writing.

A more serious erosion of the Druids' position at Stonehenge was created by those scholars who went to the other extreme in dating the monument and

The giant Merlin
building Stonehenge:
an early explanation
of the monument in a
fourteenth-century
manuscript.

Opposite: The giant
trilithon against a
starry sky was Wil-
liam Blake's image of
the Druid system of
law and science,
which brought to an
end the innocent,
poetically inspired
golden age of Jerusa-
lem in Britain, and
then spread from
these islands to cover
the whole world.
Since it was from
Britain, in Blake's
view, that the cor-
rupting influence of
man-made law and
religion first emanat-
ed, it was Britain's
destiny to make the
first reformation by
invoking again the
spirit that reigned in
the Jerusalem of
primal antiquity.

claimed that it was built before the appearance in Britain of the Celts and their
Druid priests. James Douglas in *Nenia Britannica*, 1793, was the author of the
theory that it was a pre-Celtic sun temple, which may have remained in subse-
quent use as a place of assembly down to Anglo-Saxon times. This idea received little contemporary support, but it was taken up again in Lord Avebury's *Prehistoric Times*, 1865, where Stonehenge was stated to be a pre-Celtic
temple and definitely not Druidical.

By the end of the nineteenth century, the reaction of the learned against the
Druids had become so extreme that any suggestion of their possible connection with Stonehenge was received as archaeological heresy. Druids were associated with Romanticism, with mystical philosophy, magic and the occult,
and thus with the very aspect of antiquarianism from which the newly-styled
archaeologists, as modern men of science, were most concerned to dissociate
themselves. 'Archaeologists in general have come to regard them [the Druids]
as almost unmentionable in polite society', wrote Professor Richard Atkinson
in 1965, explaining this attitude as a response to the tenacious hold retained
by the Stonehenge Druids on popular imagination and the elaborate theories
that had grown up around them. And he explained the continued popular association of Druids with Stonehenge as partly due to 'the fascination exercised
on the public mind by the idea of human sacrifice'.

Yet the public mind, having been conditioned by generations of authorities
to see Stonehenge as a temple of the Druids, could hardly be blamed if it were
somewhat less agile than that of the professors in turning against the Druid
image. And in many cases the almost personal antipathy towards the Druids,
expressed by archaeological writers, seemed no less irrational than the picturesque notions of the old antiquarians. If not the Druids, then who? was a
reasonable question, and the common response of the professors, that Stonehenge was built for an unknown purpose by an unknown race of pre-Celtic
British natives, left it essentially unanswered. Stripped of their Druids and
peopled only by the vague forms of, presumably, skin-clad, club-toting savages, the Stonehenge ruins had never before seemed so bleak and alien.

The necessary task of restoring to Stonehenge a people worthy of its architectural qualities was undertaken by an astronomer, Sir J. Norman Lockyer,
the eminent Victorian man of science and letters. Following his studies of the

Their Gods, or the spiritual Four-fold London eternal
In immense labours & sorrows, ever building, ever falling,
Thro Albions four Forests which overspread all the Earth,
From London Stone to Blackheath east: to Hounslow west:
To Finchley north: to Norwood south: and the weights
Of Enitharmons Loom play lulling cadences on the
        winds of Albion
From Caithness in the north, to Lizard-point & Dover in the south

Loud sounds the Hammer of Los, & loud his Bellows is heard
Before London to Hampsteads breadths & Highgates heights To
Stratford & old Bow: & across to the Gardens of Kensington
On Tyburns Brook: loud groans Thames beneath the iron Forge
Of Rintrah & Palamabron of Theotorm & Bromion to
        forge the instruments
Of Harvest: the Plow & Harrow to pass over the Nations

The Surrey hills glow like the clinkers of the furnace: Lambeths Vale
Where Jerusalems Foundations began: where they were laid in ruins
Where they were laid in ruins from every Nation & Oak Groves rooted
Dark gleams before the Furnace-mouth a heap of burning ashes
When shall Jerusalem return & overspread all the Nations
Return: return to Lambeths Vale O building of human souls
Thence stony Druid Temples overspread the Island white
And thence from Jerusalems ruins, from her walls of salvation
And praise: thro the whole Earth were reard from Ireland
To Mexico & Peru west, & east to China & Japan: till Babel
The Spectre of Albion frownd over the Nations in glory & war
All things begin & end in Albions ancient Druid rocky shore
But now the Starry Heavens are fled
        from the mighty limbs of
                Albion

Loud sounds the Hammer of Los, loud turn the Wheels of Enith-
Her Looms vibrate with soft affections, weaving the Web of Life
Out from the ashes of the Dead; Los lifts his iron Ladles
With molten ore: he heaves the iron cliffs in his rattling chains
From Hyde Park to the Alms-houses of Mile-end & old Bow
Here the Three Classes of Mortal Men take their fixd destinations
And hence they overspread the Nations of the whole Earth & hence
The Web of Life is woven: & the tender sinews of life created
And the Three Classes of Men regulated by Los's Hammer, and woven

One of the most magical of all Stonehenge paintings, a
view at sunset by J. W. Inchbold. *Right:* John Constable's
atmospheric view of Stonehenge with double rainbow,
painted in 1836.

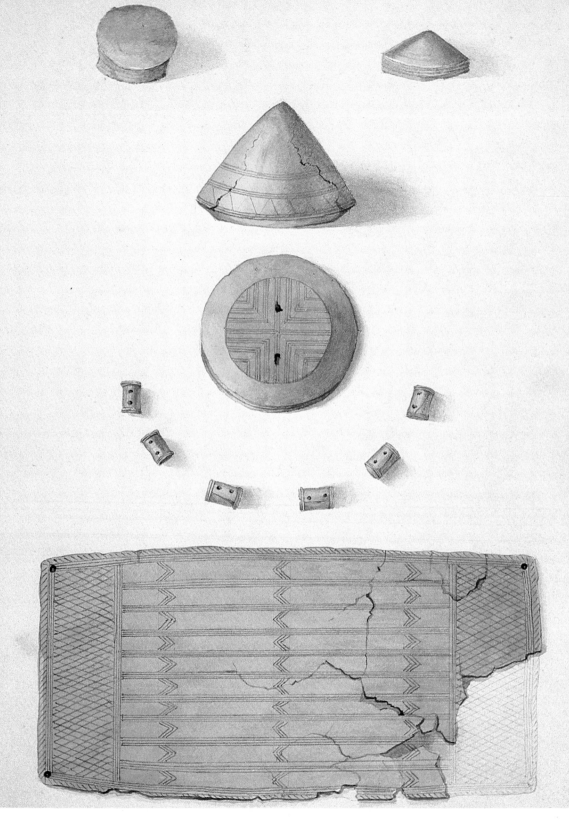

Objects of gold removed from a Wiltshire barrow early in the nineteenth century by Sir Richard Colt Hoare and recorded in the sketchbook of his antiquarian draughtsman, Philip Crocker.

astronomical orientations of Egyptian temples, Lockyer turned his attention to megalithic monuments in Britain; and with the publication in 1906 of his *Stonehenge and other British Stone Monuments Astronomically Considered*, the Druids began a furtive reoccupation of Stonehenge in the character of ancient astronomers. Lockyer identified stone circles and dolmens as the observatories and dwelling places of the ruling 'astronomer-priests' in the second and third millennia BC. These learned folk had come to Britain by sea, directly from the East, preceding by many centuries the Celtic Druids who had later inherited their science and philosophy. The Druids were 'beyond all doubt the descendants of our astronomical priests', wrote Lockyer, thus establishing their legitimate claim to Stonehenge by succession from the earlier priesthood.

Archaelogists of the now orthodox anti-Druid school closed ranks against Lockyer and his insinuating astronomer-priests. His work was denigrated and then ignored, and it was not until the 1960s, when new research confirmed the existence of an astronomical dimension in megalithic monuments, that he began to receive due recognition. Gerald Hawkins's computer study of Stonehenge, identifying sighting lines towards the extreme seasonal position of the sun and moon, caught public attention, and his book, *Stonehenge Decoded*, 1965, despite strong rearguard opposition from the archaeologists, became a bestseller. By popular acclaim the ancient astronomers, cultured and intelligent, were reinstalled in their old temple-observatory, expelling the hirsute savages of recent archaeological imagination; and the revolution was consolidated with the publication in 1967 of Professor Alexander Thom's *Megalithic Sites in Britain* in which the builders of stone circles were shown to have been adepts in geometry, number and astronomy – the very forms of scientific knowledge historically attributed to the Druids. At Stonehenge Professor Thom pointed out stone alignments and stretches of old trackways directed towards distant monuments which observers in Stonehenge could have used to mark astronomical events.

Ancient astronomers have always been the thin end of the wedge as far as the Stonehenge Druids are concerned, and once they had regained firm hold of the old stone monuments, the Druids were not long in following. We catch them in the act of creeping back as Dr Glyn Daniel, leader of the old-guard archaeological writers, admits (*Scientific American*, July 1980) that 'it is more than possible that the Druidic priesthood of the pre-Roman Celts of Gaul and Britain used them [stone circles] as temples'. There is, however, he adds, no direct archaeological evidence for this.

Archaeological evidence is not, of course, the only kind that may be considered relevant to the mystery of Stonehenge. Nor is that of the astronomers. Stonehenge is a man-made structure, designed and sited in response to human feelings and for human purposes; and as descendants of its builders, separated from them only by the small matter of some 120 generations, it is not unreasonable to suppose that our own impressions of the site might in some degree relate to those of the people who first selected it. And when it comes to feelings and impressions, the people to consult are those whose profession it is to express them – artists and poets.

In 1949 the artist, John Piper, drew and took photographs at Stonehenge and wrote an excellent article about it in *Architectural Review*, vol. 106. The reign of the anti-Druid professors was then at its height, and Piper found that the writer of the official guidebook had devoted most of his space to denunciations of 'wild and unfounded' theories, Druids, human sacrifice and so on, his

From the first book on Stonehenge, by Inigo Jones, published in 1655. The reconstructed version reflects Jones's belief that it was a temple of the Romans.

only positive statement being that Stonehenge is 'the most finished example of all Megalithic circles'.

This inadequate account, as unworthy of the public's interest as of the site itself, moved Piper to make articulate protest. He recalled how 'William Stukeley tumbled over himself with imaginative and delightful assertions', how 'John Aubrey before him was thrilled, during his lonely rides across the Plain, by the strong exhalations of humanity and worship that came from Stonehenge and Avebury', and William Long's strong impression of 'the very sacred character of the place to those who had selected this spot, and raised upon it this remarkable structure'. Today, said Piper, if we refer to the sacred atmosphere round the old stones or speculate about the people who raised them – then we are drunk and disorderly. Yet Stonehenge is one of the most beautiful man-made objects in Britain and, in relation to its site, the most awe-inspiring. Every generation sees it in a different light, and thus it continually changes, like a living thing rather than a mere archaeological monument.

In reviewing the works of the Stonehenge artists and illustrators, one might expect to find that they generally reflect the theories which were influential during the times of the artist; and so to some extent they do. Inigo Jones's Stonehenge drawings were done to illustrate his theory of its Roman origin rather than the monument as he must have seen it, and those artists who have peopled it with Druids, bards, savages or whatever have mostly done so in accordance with the opinions of their learned contemporaries. Yet many of the painters, and most of the best ones, who have worked at Stonehenge have been inspired to depict an aspect of the site which the professors have almost entirely ignored, and which Piper emphasized in his article. The common reference in many of the pictures here reproduced is to the magical or elemental quality of Stonehenge in its peculiar landscape. Generations of artists have indicated their individual perceptions of this quality by framing their Stonehenge views in tempestuous clouds, rainbows or lightning flashes.

In the most famous of all Stonehenge paintings, Constable's strange water-colour of 1835, the weird sky and light effects are considered by Louis Hawes (who wrote a fine monograph on the picture, *Constable's Stonehenge*, 1975) to re-flect the artist's own vision and state of mind rather than any particular theory or artistic convention. As a friend of the antiquarian Sir Richard Colt Hoare, who subscribed to the Druid temple view of Stonehenge, Constable must have been well informed on that and other theories current in his time, but nowhere in his surviving manuscripts is there any mention of Druids. His only refer-ence to Stonehenge scholarship is to a lecturer who tried to prove the stones antediluvian. This would have been Henry Browne, the first custodian of Stonehenge, whose book, *Illustrations of Stonehenge, Avebury*, showing that the particularly ruinous state of the south-west part of Stonehenge was due to the action of Noah's Flood which hit it from that direction, was published in 1823. Constable himself, as his writings make clear, regarded Stonehenge as a relic of unknown antiquity, far beyond the range of history or scholarship, and thus a mystery for all times.

When he began work on his Stonehenge watercolour Constable was in a state of depression, stricken by the recent death of his wife and by financial and other setbacks. He had spent time at Stonehenge making sketches for an oil painting fifteen years previously, and his return to the subject in a period of despondency may have been in response to that quality in the site which Henry James described as 'reassuring to the nerves'. That same quality was referred to again by H.G. Wells in his story, *The Secret Places of the Heart*, 1922, in which a London doctor prescribes for his world-weary patient an excursion to Stonehenge and other therapeutic shrines of the West of England. The doctor obligingly accompanies him there in his motor car, and the cure proves effective – bringing to mind one of the earliest legends of Stonehenge, that all the stones have their peculiar medicinal properties.

In Constable's lost oil painting of Stonehenge, now known only through David Lucas's mezzotint reproduction of it, the distant stones stand out against a moody sky with a crescent moon, while the sun sets behind the heel stone. Earlier, his contemporary, Turner, had painted two highly atmospher-ic views of the stones at sunrise and sunset, followed by his extraordinary scene of an elemental upheaval around Stonehenge, so violent that the shep-herd in the foreground, together with most of his flock, seems to have been struck dead by the fury of it. Thomas Girtin's watercolour of 1794 had also shown the stones under storm clouds and lightning, and the beautiful painting of 1869 by J.R. Inchbold of a sublime Stonehenge sunset provides another glimpse of the elemental powers which artists instinctively locate about these ruins.

Throughout the rises, falls and resurgences of all the various academic theories of Stonehenge, artists have been notably consistant in their comments on it; and after hearing the rival assertions and pseudo-certainties of the schol-ars, it is well to be reminded by them that the only certainty about Stonehenge is that the ancient secret it conceals is a formidable one. Anyone who pretends to have 'decoded' Stonehenge has seriously underestimated the magnitude of that task and the quality of the learning, imagination and understanding that would be required to accomplish it.

Overleaf: A strange drawing of ancient Druid activities at Stonehenge, in which Stukeley depicted the inner part of the temple as similar to Inigo Jones's earlier conception of it.

TAB. VI.

CH

Or the Scenograp

R GAVR.

Antient STONEHENGE.

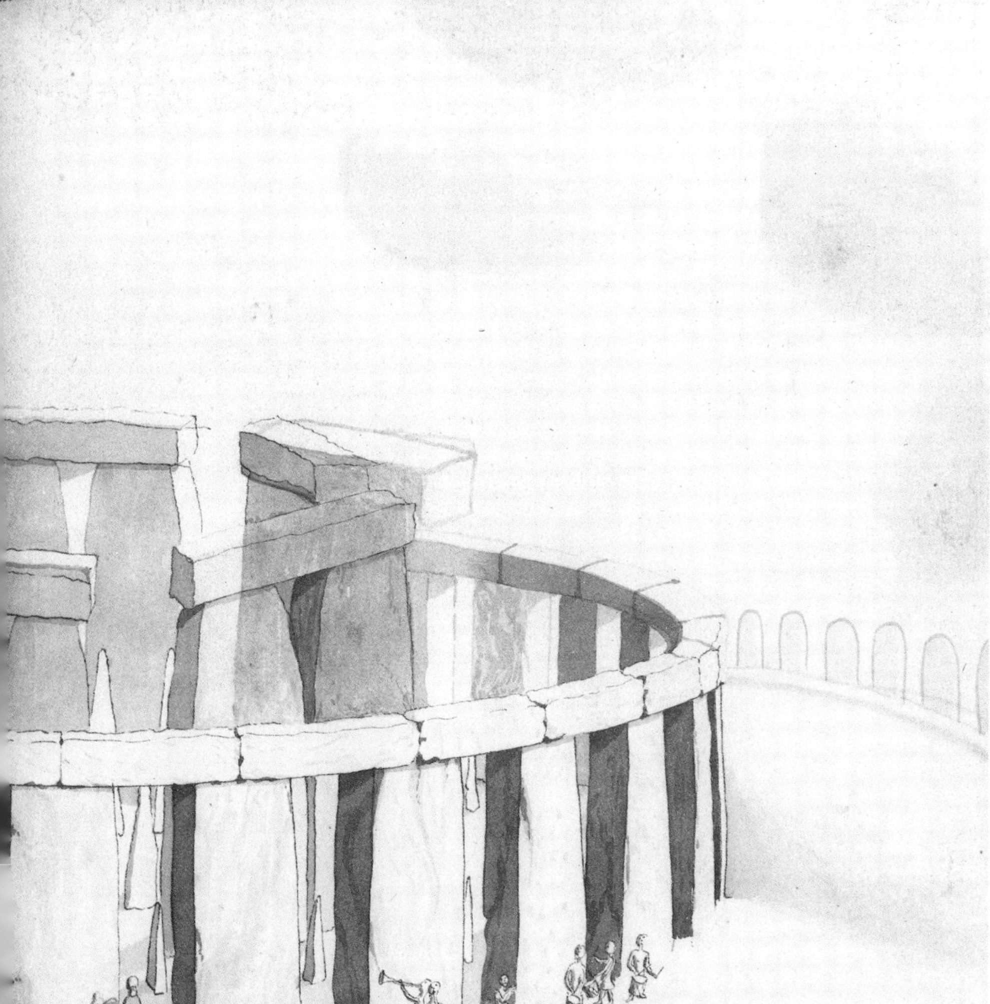

One of the most moving of Stonehenge paintings is J.M.W. Turner's
'Stonehenge at Daybreak', done in about 1816; and the most dramatic
view of the monument is the engraving after his watercolour of 1828
(*opposite, above*), in which a shepherd and most of his flock seem to have
been struck dead by the violence of an electric storm. *Opposite, below:*
Thomas Girtin's watercolour, 'Stonehenge with a Stormy Sky', painted in
1794.

Above: One of the two views of Stonehenge by the late seventeenth-century artist and engraver David Loggan, which inspired Stukeley to undertake his Stonehenge studies. The birds flying overhead have been identified as great bustards, which were then common on Salisbury Plain.

Below: To Stukeley the serpent temples of the Druid priests, spread throughout the earth, were relics of the true patriarchal religion; here, in William Blake's *Jerusalem*, they are associated with the bloody laws of authoritarian Druids who usurped the enlightened rule of the primeval Bards.

Right: John Constable's distant view of Stonehenge, painted in about 1832, is now lost, but David Lucas's mezzotint of 1843 is thought to reproduce its composition. A striking feature is its astronomical references, with the sun on the point of setting behind the heel stone while the moon rises to the left.

MEASURING THE SUN'S POSITION

At Stonehenge with the theodolite, which records
the angles with marvellous delicacy

WAITING FOR THE SUN TO RISE AT STONEHENGE, 3.30 A.M., JUNE

THE ATTEMPT TO SOLVE
THE AGE OF
STONEHENGE.

THE SUN'S PRESENT POSITION COMPARED WITH
THE AXIS OF THE BUILDING ON THE LONGEST
DAY, JUNE 21, WILL, IT IS EXPECTED, GIVE THE
DATE OF STONEHENGE.

THE FRIAR'S HEEL STONE

Looking northward. The picture also shows the
new railings to the right

Modern uses of Stonehenge, some others of which are illustrated in the last chapter of this book, have been many and diverse. *The Illustrated London News* of November 1875 (*opposite, above*) showed it as the scene of the Wiltshire Champion Coursing meeting, while in *The Sphere* of 6 July 1901 it is featured as a testing ground for the astronomical theories of Sir J. Norman Lockyer (*above and right*). The photograph on the left has the historical interest of being one of the first, in 1867, to be taken of Stonehenge. Its publication that year portended the inevitable death of the art of antiquarian illustration.

4   Archaeological illustrators and dolmen painters

Of all the antiquarian artists who have specialized in depicting megalithic monuments, personal opinion rates William Stukeley the greatest, on account of the mystical feeling for landscape that declares itself even in his detailed plans and drawings. On his antiquarian tours he took no books and consulted no authorities, preferring to draw his own conclusions from ancient sites as he found them. There were indeed very few relevant books available in his time and none at all with the number or quality of the illustrations which he included in his own. A review of previously published representations of prehistoric sites shows the extent to which he pioneered this form of illustration.

The earliest known images of Stonehenge are two which occur in fourteenth-century manuscripts, one with ancient figures gazing admiringly at the giant Merlin as he fixes one of the lintel stones to its uprights, the other absurdly representing the stone circle as a rectangle. This was the first of many poor shots at depicting Stonehenge in the centuries that followed. The next of these, a drawing by a Dutchman, Lucas de Heere, in 1574, gives a reasonable impression except that it muddles up the trilithons (so named by Stukeley) with the outer sarsen circle. The next, done the following year by an artist who signed 'R.F.', gives the stones an exaggeratedly rustic appearance with some of the lintels made cylindrical like wooden logs. It must, however, have suited contemporary notions, for it was much copied, as in the plate to the 1600 edition of Camden's *Britannia* and in Webb's *A Vindication of 'Stone-Heng Restored'*, 1665. Ten years earlier Webb had edited and published the book on Stonehenge by his father-in-law, Inigo Jones, the illustrations to which went to the opposite extreme in showing the monument as a finished example of Roman architecture. They were so inaccurate that Stukeley doubted that the great architect, who had died by the time the book came out, had much of a hand in

Webb's production. John Aubrey, however, copied one of Inigo Jones's Stonehenge drawings for his *Monumenta Britannica*. In his manuscript, which after 300 years was finally published in 1980 by Dorset Publishing Company, Aubrey included several plans and drawings of Stonehenge, Avebury and other ancient sites, among them the Rollright stones which David Loggan had previously drawn for Dr Robert Plot's *Natural History of Oxfordshire* in 1677. The same artist engraved the 'bustard' Stonehenge views which first attracted Stukeley to the monument.

Apart from these and a few other figures of prehistoric monuments in early topographical works, Stukeley's drawings of many sites in England were without precedent. For those of Wales he was able to copy the unpublished sketches, made at the end of the seventeenth century, by Edward Lhuyd, the Celtic scholar and antiquary, who also recorded and drew sites in Cornwall and Ireland. Some stone circles in the Scottish islands had previously been figured in two books, Martin Martin's *A Description of the Western Islands of Scotland*, 1703, and James Wallace's *An Account of the Isles of Orkney*, 1693. Martin had recorded an Orkney tradition that the Stenness and Ring of Brodgar stone circles were temples to the sun and moon, and this may have prompted Stukeley in his early plans of Avebury and Stanton Drew to give the separate circles solar and lunar attributions.

The dolmen at Poitiers, the Pierre Levée, used as a picnic resort and memorial tablet by local antiquarians in the sixteenth century.

In France, the dolmen at Poitiers had been described in 1532 by François Rabelais in *Pantagruel* as a place of resort for the local scholars who, 'when they have nothing else to do, pass the time by climbing up onto the stone and banqueting there with large quantities of bottles, hams and pastries, and inscribing their names on the capstone with a knife'. This was illustrated as early as 1561 in Georg Hoefnagel's *Civitates orbis terratum*. Otherwise the first archaeo-

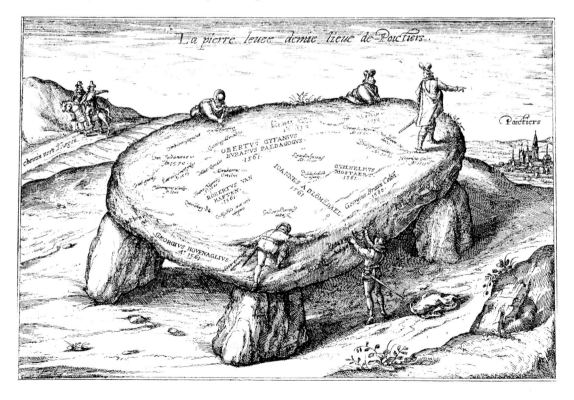

Prehistoric monu-
ments in Sweden
represented as war-
riors' tombs by Olaus
Magnus, 1555.

logical drawings of megaliths were made by Scandinavians. In his *Historia de gentibus septentrionalibus*, 1555, Olaus Magnus published a rude woodcut of some Swedish stone monuments with a detailed account of their traditional meanings as marking the tombs of different classes of Gothic warriors, whom he identified as the heroic ancestors of the modern Swedes. The idea of their country as the homeland of the legendary Goths enthused the early Swedish antiquarians, especially after King Gustav II dogmatized it as the basis for his proposed Swedish empire. According to royal proclamation Sweden was the Gothic Fatherland and the Swedish people were therefore the bravest and best of all races. Scholars were instructed to find the evidence for this, funds were provided, and the evidence duly followed. The King's tutor, Johannes Bureus, embarked in 1599 on a tour of Sweden, noting down monuments and inscriptions, forty-eight woodcuts of which were included in his *Monumenta sveogothica hactenus exsculpta*. Thus challenged, the Danes promoted their own claims to racial or cultural superiority by the glorification of their native antiquities. In opposition to Bure and the Swedish monarch, King Christian IV of Denmark advanced the nationalist antiquarian, Ole Worm, who identified many ancient monuments throughout Scandinavia as relics of the former dominance of the Danes. These monuments were comprehensively described, and some of them were illustrated, in the six books of Worm's *Monumenta danica*, 1643, which was considered for many years to be the most authoritative work on prehistoric antiquities. It had a considerable influence on early megalithic studies in Britain, where the habit of attributing ancient monuments to the Danes, begun in 1625 by Walter Charleton with his theory of a Danish Stonehenge, continued among local antiquarians for many years.

The Swedish response to Worm's antiquarian chauvinism involved a far higher claim on behalf of the Swedes than anything Worm or his colleagues had been able to produce for the Danes. In 1675 the first part of Olaus Rudbeck's *Atlantica* was published, announcing its author's discovery, from the evidence of his excavations of ancient sites near the University of Uppsala where he was a professor, that Sweden was the original Atlantis. It followed from this that Rudbeck's own native country was the source of every culture throughout the entire world. Among the expatriate Swedes of universal antiquity he listed the Scythians, Barbarians, Asians, Giants, Goths, Phrygians, Trojans, Amazons, Thracians, Libyans, Moors, Taphians, Gauls, Cimbri,

Cimmerii, Saxons, Suebians, Longobardians, Vandals, Herulians, Gepidians, Teutons, Angles, Picts, Danes, Sicambrians ... in other words the entire cast of the ancient world. Aubrey copied this list, together with one of Rudbeck's archaeological drawings, for his *Monumenta Britannica*.

Oblivious to the high-faluting claims of nationalist scholars, country people throughout Europe continued in their traditional belief that ancient giants, dwarfs or sorcerers were responsible for the prehistoric monuments of their localities. This belief was illustrated in the earliest views of the *hunebedden* or giants' beds in the province of Drenthe, which covers one of the rare districts of rising ground in Holland, by Johan Picardt in his *Korte Beschryvinge van eenige verborgene antiquiteten*, 1660. One of the beds, which consist of galleries made up of adjoining dolmens, is shown in the process of construction by an alliance of giants and dwarfs; another is attended by a tribe of noble savages like Red Indians or South Sea islanders, and a chambered mound is restored as the lodge of a shamanic priestess surrounded by the grisly offerings of her suppliants.

Similar monuments in Holland and Germany were engraved from earlier drawings in John Keysler's *Antiquitates selectae septentrionales et celticae*, published in 1720. Keysler, a German, had lived for some years in England. He knew Stonehenge, of which his was the first illustration to be shown in a foreign book, and he was a friend of Stukeley; but extensive tours of north European antiquities had weaned him from the Druid faith. He noted similarities between Stonehenge and megalithic sites in Germany, which he did not believe had ever been Druid territory, and suggested therefore that all these monuments were burial places of the Saxons.

One of the 'giants' beds' of Drenthe, Holland, figured by Picardt in 1660.

More than fifty 'giants' beds' still remain in the Dutch province of
Drenthe. Picardt in the seventeenth century heard and illustrated the
common belief that they were the work of an alliance of giants and
cunning dwarfs. He also (*below*) illustrated the association of certain local
mounds with the activities of the *Witte Wijven* or wise women who
flourished in that province until lately and were consulted as sibyls,
healers and diviners. The witches' mounds here resemble the shamanic
lodges of the North American Indians.

High standards of antiquarian illustration in Ireland were set in the eighteenth century by Thomas Wright, author of the *Louthiana*, 1748, and Gabriel Beranger, and were upheld by the distinguished artist-scholars of the next hundred years, including George Petrie, Henry O'Neill, J.H. Burgess of Ulster, G.V. Du Noyer, W.F. Wakeman, J. Windere of Cork and many others whose works are unpublished. In 1699 Edward Lhuyd had discovered New Grange, and his assistant, William Jones, had made drawings of this and other Irish antiquities both for him and for Sir Thomas Molyneux, author of *A Discourse Concerning the Danish Mounts, Forts and Towers in Ireland*, published in 1726. The Danish attribution thus given to the great chambered mounds of Ireland was justified by Molyneux as being in accordance with local traditions (which in Ireland credited giants or Danes with all ancient works) and with the evidence in Ole Worm's writings. He was not, however, infected by Worm's nationalism, an Irish variety of which was in force among some of his contemporaries. This is made plain in the rebuke he made them in his *Discourse*:

'Tho' most nations have been apt to fall into the vanity of deriving themselves from a more antient origin than truth or credible authority will vouch for; yet no people have carried this extravagance farther than the natives of *Ireland*, presuming to romance to that degree in their chronicles, as not only to deduce their stock from generations near the flood, but to invent antediluvian stories, and a fable of a niece of *Noah* himself landing in this island.'

Yet Irish nationalism was to prove an effective spur to antiquarian studies, and vice versa. In 1770 General Charles Vallancey, a military surveyor, issued the first of his six volumes of *Collectanea de rebus Hibernicis*, the illustrations to which included accurately drawn details of New Grange, referred to as a Mithraic cave. Like many others he was struck by the contrast between the wretched poverty of modern Ireland and the glories of the ancient civilization, evident in the native monuments and traditions, which he found to contain references to scientific astronomy. Such knowledge could only have come from the East, and Vallancey made learned comparisons between the Irish language and Sanscrit and between the towers, dolmens and Mithraic caves of Ireland, India and Persia, concluding vaguely that Irish culture was a product of Chaldean, Indian, African or some other form of prehistoric colonialism.

A drawing by Thomas Wright in about 1746 of an unidentified 'Sepulchral Mount near Temple Patrick in the county of Antrim'. Like New Grange and other chambered mounds in Ireland, it is surrounded by remains of a stone circle.

Pictured shortly before his death in 1835, young Henry O'Brien, the disappointed author of *The Round Towers of Ireland,* a brilliant but controversial work which failed to win the prize for which it was written.

Thus began the war of the round towers, fought by rival bands of Irish scholars over the next hundred years, the chief of the many points at issue being whether the old Irish towers, chapels and crosses were of pagan or Christian origin and whether they were colonial or native. An early casualty of the war was a brilliant youth from the west of Ireland, Henry O'Brien, who at the age of twenty-four wrote in his second language, English, a most original essay, *The Round Towers of Ireland or the History of the Tuath-de-Danaans,* proving with many references to Eastern literature that the round towers were built by Persian immigrants as fire temples in connection with serpent worship and a phallic cult. The essay was written for a prize of £50 advertised by the Royal Irish Academy in 1830. The Academy's Committee awarded the prize to one of their own members, George Petrie, who argued the Christian origin of the towers. O'Brien protested fiercely, stirring up opposition to his cause as well as support for it, and died disappointed at the age of twenty-seven.

The prizewinner, Petrie, was a trained artist and keen antiquarian, and he so dominated the field of antiquarian and topographical book illustration during the first part of the nineteenth century that scarcely an illustrated work was published in Ireland to which he had not contributed. His orthodox views gained him official posts, as antiquarian artist to the Academy and director of the historical department of the Ordnance Survey of Ireland. Authorities of both Church and State preferred his identification of the round towers as belfries and places of refuge of early Christians to the more exciting theories of those who claimed them as pagan works, because the latter had become associated with radical nationalism. Petrie's colleague, Henry O'Neill the 'dolmen painter', who upheld the pagan theory, was the author of a pamphlet, *Ireland for the Irish*, attacking landlordism, and this gained him enemies in high places. When his book *The Most Interesting of the Ancient Crosses of Ancient Ireland* came out in 1857, important members of the Academy, including Sir William Wilde, refused to subscribe to it on the specious grounds that O'Neill's artistic, finely detailed lithographs of the crosses were inacccurate.

In 1833 Petrie obtained his Ordnance Survey post to assist in a grand scheme for publishing maps of each of the Irish counties together with books descriptive of their ancient monuments, customs and traditions, natural history and geology. Some distinguished and patriotic Irish scholars were engaged in the project, including two antiquarians, John O'Donovan and Eugene O'Curry, who were former hedge schoolmasters (successors to the teachers of the Irish bardic schools suppressed in 1641, who continued to instruct children in Irish literature, Greek and Latin, astronomy, navigation and other subjects in the ancient curriculum until their pupils were forcibly removed from them by the imposition of compulsory 'education' in English in 1831). Much interesting material was collected relating to antiquities and local lore, but only one of the proposed volumes had been published when the Government abruptly put a stop to the project by withdrawing its funds. The reason, as generally understood at the time, was that the revival of interest in Irish antiquities was encouraging nationalistic sentiment.

The grand controversies and petty quarrels which have characterized Irish antiquarianism seem also to have heightened its interest, attracting many lively scholars to the subject and some accomplished artists. For these a further, more practical attraction was the chance of illustrating the guidebooks to picturesque or antiquarian travels which came into fashion towards the end of the eighteenth century. Petrie, O'Neill, Wakeman and Burgess were among the Irishmen who profited from this trend. Similar contributions to illustrated books on Brittany were made by the French painters, Jean-Baptiste Jorand and Félix Benoist. In England, following the popular success of Stukeley's

Henry O'Neill's picture of the ancient Irish sanctuary, Monasterboice in County Louth, with its round tower and crosses.

'Druidical remains' had become popular subjects by the end of the eighteenth century to illustrators of topographical books, who were inclined to exaggerate their size and hoary rustic appearance. This is apparent in the engraving, published in 1801, from Sir Richard Colt Hoare's sketch of the three stones at Trellech, Monmouthshire.

Stonehenge and *Abury,* professional artistic and literary tourists, such as Pennant, Hearne, Britton and many others, took to ornamenting their books with megalithic views, Stonehenge being easily the favourite subject. Throughout the nineteenth century it was a subject of constant interest to painters, including the great names mentioned in the previous chapter and a host of their notable contemporaries, reflecting the ever-increasing appeal of megalithic sites to scholars and the general public alike. One of the best patrons of antiquarian artists and writers was Sir Richard Colt Hoare of Stourhead in Wiltshire. He was himself a competent artist, although with a weakness, shared by many of his contemporaries, for conveying the impressive aspect of 'rude stone monuments' by exaggerating their size in comparison with the human figure. To draw ancient sites and objects from Wiltshire barrows for the plates to his magnificent volumes of *Ancient Wiltshire,* published between 1812 and 1820, Hoare engaged Philip Crocker, a draughtsman with the Ordnance Survey, who, given the opportunity, made his name as the leading antiquarian artist of his time.

Before the days of modern travel, artists would tour the country on foot or horseback, making sketches of local views and antiquities, some of which might be engraved to illustrate published works. The best of Stukeley's plates were engraved by Gerard Vandergucht or John Pine, both of whom were members of his Order of Roman Knights and rode with him on several antiquarian tours. Their skill at converting Stukeley's quick sketches and notes into finished, detailed engravings was matched by many of their nineteenth-century successors. When Gilbert White saw the drawings which the illustrator of his *Natural History of Selborne,* S. Hieronymus Grimm, was about to send off to the engraver, he was surprised at how slight they were, but Grimm assured him that they were adequate for the purpose, and so it turned out. Illustrations for topographical books were much in demand, and there was keen competition among artists to supply them. Looking through archaeological

The first book of North American archaeology was Squier and Davis's
Ancient Monuments of the Mississippi Valley, published in 1847. The two
pioneer authors viewed and surveyed some of the vast number of mounds
and earthworks in the Mid-West, many of which have since been
obliterated. Among the fine detailed engravings illustrating their work are
(*above*) a general view of some of the 'mounds of sepulture' they
encountered on their travels, and (*below*) a glimpse of high summer at a
settlement by the great mound at Grave Creek. In 1838 this mound was
excavated, and among the wonderful ornaments and artefacts found within
was the famous Grave Creek tablet (figured on page 144).

books and journals up to about 1880, one is struck by the quality of the engravings that illustrate them. Many of these were by antiquarians who drew and engraved the plates for their own books. Others were by professional illustrators, rarely acknowledged and often sadly exploited. John Thomas Blight of Penzance charged as little as five shillings for a small but detailed wood-engraving, and during his short career, terminated in 1871 by madness due to excessive work and worry, he claimed never to have earned as much as £100 in any year. From the 1860s onwards the highly developed skills of the engravers in wood, steel and stone became gradually obsolete with the advancement of photography. The *camera lucida* was a boon to archaeological draughtsmen, and so at first was the photographic camera. Some of the finest engravings of old stone monuments were made from photographs. But in 1867 Colonel Sir Henry James, Director of the Ordnance Survey, published a book which contained eight of the earliest photographs to be taken of Stonehenge, and the monopoly of the artists was broken. There followed a rapid plunge in the standards of archaeological illustration as dim photographs replaced the work of the highly trained draughtsmen. There is beauty and interest in some of the early photographic views of ancient monuments and the goings-on around them, but it is only in the last few years, with the improvement of techniques of photography and printing, that the camera has begun to make amends for the skills and talents extinguished by its invention.

Few painters until recently have specialized in prehistoric monuments as narrowly as did Richard Tongue or Tonge of Bath, who described himself as 'painter and modeller of megaliths'. Only a few of Tongue's large, grave canvases have been located, but he is known to have worked around the 1830s in Brittany, Cornwall and Wales as well as at Stonehenge. Louis Hawes in his review of Stonehenge painters (in his *Constable's Stonehenge*) calls Tongue 'irretrievably obscure' and his work 'decidedly mediocre', but he certainly knew how to show off a stone. He went directly for the object he meant to depict, and

The Motte Stone on the Isle of Wight, a local landmark to which many legends have been attached, illustrated in 1816.

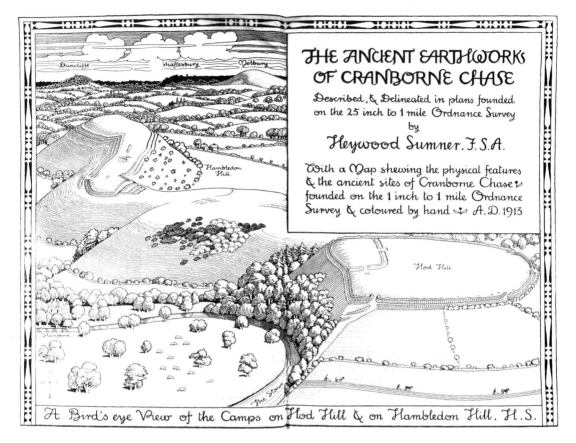

THE ANCIENT EARTHWORKS
OF CRANBORNE CHASE
Described, & Delineated in plans founded
on the 25 inch to 1 mile Ordnance Survey
by
Heywood Sumner. F.S.A.

With a Map shewing the physical features
& the ancient sites of Cranborne Chase
founded on the 1 inch to 1 mile Ordnance
Survey & coloured by hand ⚬ A.D. 1913

A Bird's eye View of the Camps on Hod Hill & on Hambledon Hill. H.S.

With his archaeological drawings made early this century, Heywood Sumner revived the old tradition of depicting ancient sites in relation to their natural surroundings. Shown here, in bird's eye view, are some of the earthworks of Cranborne Chase, Dorset.

his megalithic landscapes by virtue of their size and simplicity are more impressive than comparable work by more respected artists.

As previously illustrated in the case of the Stonehenge painters, many artists have independently chosen to represent megalithic sites in accordance with their folklore and with the impressions recorded by many of the old antiquarians as places of elemental magic. Most awesome of all megalithic images are those created by Caspar David Friedrich of the 'giants' beds' in north Germany, in which the solid permanence of the stones, venerable sanctuaries in the days of the Nordic sagas, contrasts with the shivering transience of their mundane surroundings. In these pictures the old monuments are not merely symbols of mysterious antiquity, as for instance was the pastiche of Stonehenge in Thomas Jones's *Bard* painting, but locations of the eternal spirit of the land, personified in the ancient gods and heroes. A very different form of the native spirit, that of the Irish countryside, is represented in the painting of an Irish dolmen by 'A.E.' (the mystical poet George Russell), in which is also shown the agitation of elemental forces round the monument spoken of by dowsers and seers. This approach to megalith painting has been revived within the last few years by the many young painters who have been inspired by the wide range of possible interpretations opened up by modern archaeological discoveries. Among the few represented here are Richard Caston, Christopher Castle, John Glover, and Paul Devereux, whose quarterly magazine, *The Ley Hunter*, expresses many of the ideas referred to by these painters.

Fig. I. b) Prospectus ejus
è meridionali latere.

Monumentum Salisburiense vulgò
STONE HENGE dictum.

Fig. II. ad Sect. I. c. I. §. 3

Moles Saxeæ in Drenthiâ.

Above, left: A view of Stonehenge by a German traveller, J.G. Keysler, illustrated his book of 1720, in which were also figures (*left*) of megalithic monuments in Holland and north Germany. In defiance of Stukeley he insisted that all these structures were Saxon tombs, not Druid temples.

Fig. V. ad Sect. I. c. 3. §. 3.

Ara gentilis Albersdorffensis in Holsatiâ.

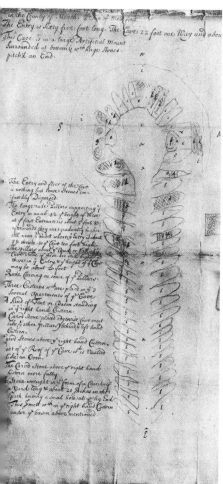

Above: a section of the passage and inner chamber at New Grange from Vallancey's book of 1786. Vallancey identified the mound as an ancient sun-temple, dedicated to Mithras.

Below, left: The interior of New Grange; a plan drawn by William Jones in 1700.

Below: a drawing by Gabriel Beranger in 1775 of Dowth, the great mound near New Grange. The building on top was a tea house, which had recently been put there by an eccentric of the district, Lord Netterville.

Above: A characteristic eighteenth-century image by the watercolourist, Moses Griffith, of an ancient bard vaticinating at the Bachwen cromlech in the region of Mount Snowdon, Caernarvonshire.

Right: In 1787, a few years after Captain Cook's visit to Easter Island in the south-east Pacific, the French global navigator, the Comte de la Pérouse, spent twenty-four hours there investigating the giant monolithic statues, many of which at that time were still erect. Perhaps because of the theft of his hat, illustrated in this engraving, he found the natives 'as corrupt as the circumstances in which they are placed will allow them to be'.

Below: Part of a large oil painting by the 'dolmen painter', Richard Tongue of Bath, done in 1830, of a despairing figure at Pentre Ifan, sometimes called Arthur's Quoit, in Pembrokeshire.

Right: Two engravings from Philip Crocker's drawings of the great stones and circular earthwork at Avebury, used to illustrate Colt Hoare's *Ancient Wiltshire* (1812-20).

Above: A tumulus or 'giant's grave' in the snow (*Hünengrab im Schnee*) by Caspar David Friedrich (1774-1840). Friedrich captured the intense, other-worldly atmosphere surrounding the ancient sites of the north German landscape. A similar effect (*right*) is achieved in Paul Devereux's recent painting of Wayland's Smithy, a ruined barrow on the Berkshire downs. *Opposite:* The cromlech at Gwernvale near Crickhowel, Brecon, a sepia drawing of about 1832 by Pryce Carter Edwards (*above*); pilgrims at Clonmacnoise, by George Petrie (*below*). As his view of the Christianized prehistoric sanctuary in County Offaly shows, Petrie shared in the sentiment for the lost glories of ancient Ireland which led to the revival of interest in indigenous culture and, ultimately, to the modern resurgence of Irish nationalism.

Opposite, above: Thomas Jones, who painted 'The Bard' in 1774, had previously paid a visit to Stonehenge and was impressed by the 'grandeur and magnificence' of its setting, 'the surrounding Void not affording any thing to disturb the Eye or divert the imagination'. Transferring its ruined trilithons to a Welsh mountain landscape of blasted oaks and Druidic rocks, he made them symbols of the decline and fall of the ancient Bardic order, as described by his poetic contemporary, Thomas Gray. The influence of Stukeley and of the poems of Ossian are apparent in this tragic monument to the glories of British antiquity.

Above: A fine nineteenth-century steel engraving of Kit's Coty House in Kent, by E. Penstone.

Left: Cow Castle on Exmoor, near Simonsbath, Somerset, painted by George Cumberland in about 1820. This strange site consists of an isolated, conical rock, its summit encircled by a stone rampart about seven feet high. Describing it in his *Ancient Earthworks of Somerset*, 1924, E.J. Burrow wrote: 'It is difficult to see what purpose such an inclosure served, overlooked as it is on all sides, and in a very exposed position, with a precipitous fall inside the inclosure.'

Henry O'Neill (see page 47) made his name in mid-nineteenth-century Ireland as an antiquarian scholar and meticulous illustrator of ancient monuments. Some of these he also recorded on large canvases. *Above* is his oil painting of the great dolmen at Proleek, County Louth.

Left: An Irish dolmen, painted early this century by the mystic, 'A.E.' (George Russell). The nature of his visions at the sacred places of old Ireland, described in his poetic writings, is suggested by the attendant figure and the swirling, multi-coloured energy patterns surrounding the ancient stone. Title of the painting: 'So the Vision Flamed and Fled'.

Right: Sketches of Irish monuments from the notebook of Henry O'Neill, made in 1851.

Cromlech on Mount Venus

Dec. 31st 1851

Cromlech at Brennanstown Co Dublin
Dec 25th 1851

South Side Dec 25th 1851   *Cromlech near Shanganagh Co Dubl.*

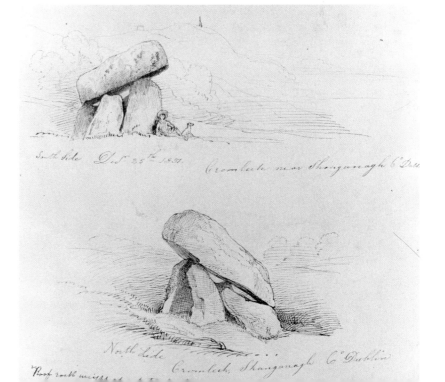

North Side

Cromlech, Shanganagh Co Dublin

Roof rock missing

The Scottish painter William Nesfield's 'Circle of Stones at Tormore, Isle of Arran' was exhibited in London in 1828. The haunted atmosphere of the old stones, here enhanced by weird light from a thundery sky, is constantly referred to by artists at megalithic sites.

In mundane contrast, but often of great appeal and historical interest, are the unsophisticated records of ancient monuments by local artists, such as James Moore's 1849 view (*below*) of the Kempe Stones near Dundonald, County Down.

Right: Sketches of a Welsh dolmen near Login, Pembrokeshire, made in the 1970s by John Piper, who was one of the first of the modern painters of ancient sites to dispute the exclusive right of archaeologists to interpret megalithic monuments.

5   Sketches at Carnac

Around Carnac, a seaside village in the department of Morbihan, southern Brittany, is the most amazing collection of megalithic monuments to be found anywhere in the world. It contains some of the largest and strangest relics of prehistoric antiquity, including the most mysterious of all, the famous Carnac alignments. These consist of four groups of upright stones, arranged in parallel alignments, each set of alignments running at a slightly different angle towards the north-east. From the huge boulders at their western termini the rows regularly diminish in size towards the east, ending with stones no more than two or three feet high. The thin, sandy soil of the district gives little support to the stones, which are mostly balanced on the underlying rock. Many of them have fallen or been removed, even in quite recent times, for building or road-making. Most of the survivors were re-erected at the end of the nineteenth century and, whether on this account or as originally designed, the rows are not perfectly straight but undulate along their course like serpents.

Stretching for over two miles through heather and pine woods, these armies of stones are among the great wonders of the world. Many writers have described their sensations on first sight of them, and artists have commonly exaggerated their size and density in attempts to convey their striking appearance. Not to be outdone, the scholars and scientists have produced a quite remarkable range of theories about Carnac which have enlivened its modern history at least as much as they have illuminated its past.

The first disciplined observer to record Carnac, in 1725, was the Marquis de Robien, president of the Breton parliament and the owner of a large estate in the district, who left an unpublished account of the stones, together with several fine drawings, all of which are in the Municipal Library at Rennes. After describing some of the theories already in the field, he concluded soberly

A general view of the Carnac alignments, 1850.

that 'all one can say is that this work represents a prodigious amount of labour, and it must have needed an incredible multitude of people to carry it out'. Such a restrained comment is rarely found in the works of the Carnac experts. Earlier, as Robien reports, M. de La Sauvagère had been led by the local name, Caesar's Camp, to identify the aligned stones as giant tent pegs or poles, set up by Caesar's army to preserve their shelters from the strong local winds. The occasion of this was the Roman conquest of the nation of the Veneti, whose powerful navy was thought to have been defeated in the bay opposite Carnac. M. Deslandes had suggested that the stones had been set up by the action of the Flood, and others believed that they monumentalized the lines of a famous battle or commemorated its slain heroes. This military theme reflected the traditional local explanation of the stone rows as being columns of Roman soldiers miraculously petrified by Carnac's patron saint, St Cornély, whom they had pursued to his own shores after evicting him from the papal throne in Rome. He was also the patron saint of cattle, and a bull cult still lingers at Carnac where the parish church displays an image of the saint blessing two paintings of bulls surrounded by menhirs and dolmens. The antiquity of this cult is evidenced by the bones of cattle found in association with prehistoric burials and by the statue of a bull excavated from a Roman villa near Carnac. Every year on the saint's feast day, September 13, the local farmers still bring their cattle up to the church, where they are blessed and then paraded through the streets. The astrologically minded have seen this as a survival from the Age of Taurus, the start of which preceded the Christian or Piscean era by some 4,000 years, thus giving a date for the stones which roughly coincides with modern archaeological estimates.

An early interpretation of the Carnac stones, by Count de Caylus (in his

Recueil des antiquités..., 1761–67), made them the monuments of an unknown race of seafarers who settled for a time on the coasts of Brittany, driving the native Gauls into the interior, and then went on to Britain, where they erected similar monuments as permanent reminders to posterity of their presence there. Fifty years later these people were positively identified as the ancient Egyptians. The man who discovered this was an antiquarian-minded Royalist naval officer, Count Maudet de Penhouët. He applied to Carnac the same methods as had been used by Stukeley at Avebury, and thus arrived at the same conclusion: that the Carnac alignments were another example of a dracontium, a temple representing the deity in the form of a serpent. In the serpentine avenues of Carnac he recognized symbols of ancient Egyptian hermetic philosophy, and further evidence of an Egyptian presence in prehistoric Brittany revealed itself in the monuments and place names of the local countryside. In the grounds of the castle at Quinipily he found an antique statue of Isis, and he derived the name Carnac from Karnak, the site of the famous Egyptian temple which is approached by a line of sphinxes, reminiscent of the lines of stones at the Breton temple.

Maudet de Penhouët's *Essai sur les monumens armoricains* was published in 1805, and that same year his notions of Brittany's Egyptian origins received a spirited challenge from a scholar of very different political sympathies, a revolutionary nationalist, Jacques de Cambry. His *Monumens celtiques* was dedicated to Napoleon, congratulating him on planting the French flag on the Pyramids, and offering him a description of 'the oldest, greatest monument in the world', the Druid temple at Carnac. This remarkable book begins with the declaration that the Celts, Gauls and Franks are one and the same people, and goes on to show that they were the first civilized race, that their high culture was copied by all other nations, and that Breton is the only pure language and was the source of all the rest. All this had been ignored by French scholars who, so Cambry complained, were ever willing to praise other nations at the expense of their own and to attribute to alien peoples the megalithic monuments which in fact proved the pre-eminent ancient glories of France. If Carnac were situated near London, he declared, it would have been made famous all over the world through the works of English painters and poets, for it was known that the British government found the money for the expensively produced books on Stonehenge and encouraged artists to make engravings of it. These engravings were carried by the English to the most distant continents, and from them they derived their sense of confidence and cultural superiority. This was all very well, said Cambry, but in fact the English had taken their entire culture, their arts, crafts, forms of government and law and every one of their civilized institutions, from the French. Even the name of their country, Britannia, was taken from the Bretons. Among the appalling statues of London the least bad were done by Frenchmen, and the English only had the fire engine because it was introduced by a French refugee.

From this outburst Cambry turned to examine the stones of Carnac as relics of those founders of universal culture, the Celtic Druids. The stones, he found, had to do with astronomy. The ancient Druids would observe the motions of the heavens and interpret them to the people, thus achieving a divinely ordered society. He reckoned that part of the alignments near Carnac, at Le Ménec, was intended to represent the signs of the zodiac, a stone row to every sign. He was disconcerted at being able to count only eleven rows, but then he read somewhere that the ancient zodiac contained only eleven signs. Modern surveys of Le Ménec show that it was in fact made up of twelve stone rows.

Engraving from
Cambry's book of
1805 showing part of
the stone rows at
Erdeven to the north-
west of Carnac.

The purpose of Cambry's book was to raise the nationalistic spirit of post-revolutionary France by creating a revised version of history in which the natural superiority of the French people was illustrated by the country's traditions and megalithic monuments. Similar attempts by politically motivated antiquarians in the sixteenth and seventeenth centuries on behalf of the Swedes and Danes have been referred to previously (see page 42), and the historical link between antiquarianism and nationalism in Ireland has also been mentioned. The study of this constant association is a fascinating one, all the more so in that there is but a thin borderline between antiquarian research as a stimulus to local and national culture and its use in the interests of racial chauvinism. Its use for the latter purpose four hundred years ago by the empire-building King of Sweden was paralleled in modern times during the 1930s and 1940s, when German professors discovered the astronomical and geometrical properties of their ancient monuments and were encouraged by the ruling doctrines of national socialism to proclaim that their ancestors, and consequently they themselves, were of the race whose stock was superior to all others for being the most anciently civilized. The tedious recurrence of 'pre-historic nationalism' is again illustrated in a new book, *The Russian Paradox*, by two émigré Russian scholars in America, E. Klepikova and V. Solovyov, which reports the rise of an assertive form of nationalism, with the familiar trappings of xenophobia and antisemitism, within the Soviet Union. At the centre of this movement, according to the authors, is *Rossiya*, the All-Russian Association of Patriotic Societies, a body which is officially concerned with the preservation of ancient monuments.

All this is a very different sort of nonsense from the megalithic revivalism of Stukeley, whose attempt to raise the spirit of his nation by emphasizing its high traditions was but the first stage in his greater programme for a world-wide restoration of ancient religious principles. Cambry's tone was more hectoring and chauvinistic than Stukeley's, but in his vision of the wisdom and nobility of the old Celtic Druids, and in his identification of his own country as their natural motherland and citadel, he was obviously akin to his English predecessor. The effect of his writing was also similar to that of Stukeley's. As was Stonehenge to the mystical patriots of England, so Carnac became to the French. It was regarded as a settled fact that the Celts of Brittany in their greatest days had erected the stones for use as a temple, and learned men turned to filling out the more intimate details in the emerging picture of these people's way of life. Canon Mahé of Vannes concluded that the spaces between the sets of alignments at Carnac had been occupied by the Druids' houses, where they lived in pious domesticity with their wives and children, instructing numerous pupils from among the nobility, and providing lodgings for the pilgrims attending Carnac's religious festivals. Researches of this sort were encouraged by the learned *Académie celtique*, founded in 1805. Its declared objects were to promote studies of the Celtic language and of all other languages, particularly French, which derived from it, and to record and find explanations for the monuments of ancient Gaul.

By this time, French poets, writers and painters were beginning, as Cambry hoped they would, to emulate their allegedly government-assisted colleagues in England by turning their attention to megalithic monuments and the mysteries and splendours of their past. Impetus to this movement was given by the translation into French of James Macpherson's Ossian writings. His compilation of heroic verses, attributed to an ancient warrior bard and salvaged from the memories of old Gaelic speakers in the Scottish Highlands and Western Isles, caused a greater sensation on the Continent than it did in England, where Dr Johnson and other scholars conspired to denounce it as a forgery. Artists and poets everywhere were more impressed by the content of Ossian's, or Macpherson's, compositions than by the objections of the professors. The doings of Fingal, Cuthullin and other such representatives of ancient Celtic high culture were much celebrated in Romantic literature, and in answer to Ossian, the French in 1839 produced the *Barzaz-Breiz*, said to be a collection of the genuine old verses of Brittany. These in turn were dismissed as fakes, an opinion which is now being questioned.

Reacting against the excesses of the 'celtomaniacs', scholars began to question all the theories and assumptions which associated Druids and ancient Celtic heroes with megalithic monuments. The *Académie celtique* was reformed in 1814 as the *Société royale des antiquaires de France*, and in 1827 M. le chevalier de Fréminville began the rout of Cambry's astronomical Druids from their temple at Carnac.

Fréminville's wonderful descriptions and lively drawings of Carnac are contained in the first volume of his *Antiquités de la Bretagne*, where he attacks all the theories of his imaginative predecessors, from La Sauvagère to Cambry, before concluding that the Carnac stones were 'the tombs of warriors killed in a memorable battle, the outcome of which was of the utmost importance'. He fully agreed with Cambry's assertion that it was absurd to attribute Carnac to any foreign race, thus striking at Maudet de Penhouët, Caylus, serpent temples and ancient Egyptian colonists, but he then turned on Cambry for giving Carnac a 'celestial theme'. Excavations, he claimed, had almost always proved standing stones to have been grave markers. Of this he found further proof in the works of Ossian.

However, the world of Carnac scholarship had not yet heard the last of Maudet de Penhouët and the Carnac dracontium. That embattled veteran, who had commanded a ship in the American war of 1788, fought for his king against the revolutionary army in Brittany, and survived for a further spell of service under the restored monarchy, was still active around Carnac when it

The ancient Salt Hill at Slough was the scene of a triennial festival, Ad Montem, held by the boys of nearby Eton College. Money was levied from onlookers, the tradition being that it was for the purchase of salt, and was donated to the Senior Scholar of the year. The origin of the Montem ceremony is supposed to be coeval with the foundation of the College in 1440, in continuation of a monkish procession which took place annually to the mound, when consecrated salt was sold to the spectators. This print was published in 1838, and six years later the intrusion of a railway line and increased rowdiness at the festival led to it being abandoned. Here the ceremonies are attended by the young Queen Victoria with retinue and carriages.

A shaft of light strikes through the bardic circle at Boscawen-un,
Cornwall: a painting of 1981 by the modern megalith painter, Christopher
Castle.

The southern extremity of the stone rows at Erdeven, figured in 1827 by Fréminville, who believed that all the thousands of erect stones in the Carnac district marked the tombs of warriors killed in some great battle.

was visited in September 1831 by an English antiquarian, the Rev. John Bathurst Deane. By happy coincidence this man was a follower of Stukeley, well acquainted with the dracontium at Avebury, and on his first trip to Britanny he met the leading authority on the dracontium at Carnac. Deane spoke little French and no Breton. Maudet de Penhouët, having spent four years of his youth in England following his American campaign, was fluent in the three languages, and he offered his services as Deane's guide. 'He glories in being a Breton of pure and ancient descent', wrote Deane. It turned out, however, that General Maudet de Penhouët had commanded royalist forces in that very district against the republicans during the Reign of Terror, and that he had also commanded the gendarmerie of Rennes under Charles X. Consequently, said Deane, he was a marked man to Louis-Philippe's police, and 'we were accordingly beset by spies, followed, pursued, interrogated, and annoyed to such an extent that we were glad to make our visit a short one'.

The following year Mr Deane returned to Carnac. This time old General Maudet de Penhouët was unable to meet him, 'having heard on good authority, that if he ever ventured into that country again, he would be arrested as a Carlist'. Despite being without an interpreter in a land where few people spoke anything but Breton, Deane accomplished the purpose of his visit, which was to assist Mr Murray Vicars of Exeter, a surveyor whom he had commissioned to draw up an accurate plan of the Carnac stone alignments. This was the first time such a thing had been done.

Another useful English contribution to the records of Carnac was made by friends of Deane, a prim couple of antiquarian artists, Mr Alexander Blair and Dr Francis Ronalds. Ronalds had invented an instrument, described in his pamphlet, *Mechanical Perspective*, which served to promote accuracy in drawing, and the 24 plates in their *Sketches at Carnac*, 1834, give the best contemporary views of some of the Carnac monuments. This slim volume, containing Vicars's plan together with a brief account of Carnac and the barbaric state of the local lodging houses, was published in a small private edition and given away to a few friends and other interested people.

As if to contradict Cambry's belief that the British would only illustrate monuments that reflected glory on their own nation, another notable intervention by English scholars at Carnac was made in the 1860s. Two of the finest antiquarian surveyors of their time, the Rev. W.C. Lukis and Sir Henry Dryden, spent several seasons there together, during which they made meticulous plans and drawings of the Carnac alignments and most of the neighbouring monuments, with some vivid watercolours of the stones added by Dryden. Only a fraction of their vast works here and throughout Britain has ever been published, but their Carnac plans are highly valued by modern archaeologists because they were made before the start of the great campaign of re-erecting fallen stones which took place at the end of their century. Most of these restorations were made by Zacharie Le Rouzic, the greatest of the modern Carnac scholars and founder of the Miln-Le Rouzic museum there – the name he generously added to his own being that of the pioneer of scientific excavation at Carnac, James Miln, a Scotchman. Le Rouzic marked with a small red cement plug each of the stones which he re-erected, but there is still confusion, for Alexander Thom was told, during one of his expeditions to survey Carnac in the 1970s, that Le Rouzic would also mark stones which he believed had been re-erected earlier, and he left no written explanation of his method. Many of the stones have been wrongly placed in restoration, and in some cases Lukis's survey is the only good record of what is original.

Lukis's and Dryden's Carnac plans were rediscovered by Richard Atkinson (whose appreciative account of their work is contained in a collection of essays, *To Illustrate the Monuments*, 1976), and were made available to Professor Thom to assist his own survey. Another useful document to turn up was a plan of the alignments made by some German army surveyors to while away time during the last war. With these for reference, Professor Thom and assistants, who were mostly members of his own family, made five expeditions to Carnac, during which they achieved one of the greatest of all feats of archaeological surveying, the completion of a highly accurate survey of the Carnac alignments and of all the greater monuments in the district. This was done despite the difficulties in the modern landscape, among which the Thom family encountered 'almost impenetrable woodland', dense undergrowth now concealing many monuments, and 'an unfortunate experience with an irate peasant', as mentioned in his book, *Megalithic Remains in Britain and Brittany*, 1978.

From the evidence of his survey Thom drew two main conclusions. First, the Carnac alignments, for all the irregularities now evident in them, were originally planned as series of straight lines or geometrical arcs. From a statistical examination of the distances between the stones he found that the unit of measure used by their designers was the 'megalithic rod' of 6.8 feet, which is two and a half times the length of the unit he had already identified in the plans of British stone circles, the 'megalithic yard' of 2.72 feet. This result, being based on statistics, has invited and received the criticism of rival statisticians. These people who, like lawyers, can argue whatever side of an issue suits their purpose, have recently, with some amusing results, begun to take an interest in archaeology. Their intervention in 'ley hunting' is described in a later chapter. In Thom's book his statistical opponents are firmly taken to task for their quibbling, unphilosophical approach to evidence and for their refusal to incorporate the principle of reason within their elaborate mathematical theories. No doubt, like all the antiquarian battles ever fought at Carnac, or at Stonehenge, this one will continue.

The second important issue raised by Thom's work at Carnac concerns the inter-relationships of all the monuments in the district and their astronomical bearings. This aspect of his work, referred to again in the following chapter, is now changing the direction and emphasis of Carnac studies. Cambry's 'celestial theme' is revived, and the age of digging into tombs for clues to the meaning of Carnac gives way to the age of searching the skies for whatever it was that so interested the ancient astronomers. Yet for all the labours, speculations and scientific skills which have been applied to Carnac, its mystery remains intact, and no one who looks down those rows of great stones, stretching to the horizon, has cause to think himself much wiser than the local peasants who call them petrified soldiers.

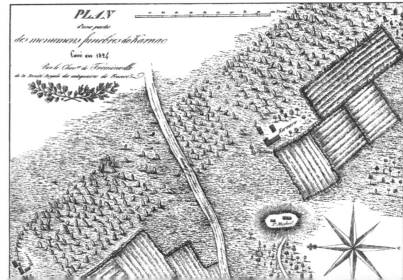

Pl. 4.

In the background of Cambry's 1805 view of his party surveying the stones of Carnac he shows a naval engagement, which he claimed to have witnessed, in which a British man-of-war was engaged and defeated by French naval vessels.

Below: Plan and prospect of some of the *monuments funèbres* at Carnac, together with some antique locals, as seen and imagined by Fréminville in 1824.

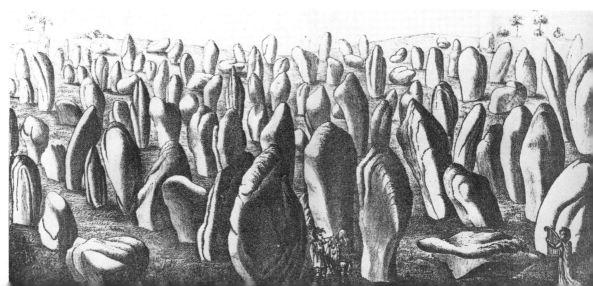

Above: The Fairies' Rock near Tanzey (Ille-et-Vilaine), figured by Maudet de Penhouët, who attributed the megalithic monuments of Brittany to ancient Egyptian colonists.

Right: Two views after Jorand, published in 1831, of the ruined stone ring at the west end of the Le Ménec alignments and, *below,* the 'grotto' at Locmariaquer.

Below: Croix de la Montagne de la Justice. Jorand's view (1831) of the curiously inscribed stone beside the path taken by early visitors to the Carnac alignments.

Lith. de Engelmann rue Louis Le grd

Two of the meticulous illustrations by the Englishmen, Blair and Ronalds, of the Carnac stones in 1834. On the left they measure one of the great stones near the village of Sainte-Barbe, and on the right is their view eastwards down the alignments at Kerlescan.

Below: Nodier and Taylor's prospect of Carnac in 1845.

Above: Photograph of 1910 showing part of the long stone rows at Kermario, east of Carnac (Morbihan), and the Dolmen de Crucuno to the north of the village. *Right:* One of the water-colours of monuments in the Carnac district painted by Sir Henry Dryden in the 1860s while engaged with the Rev. W.C. Lukis in surveying the alignments.

Blair and Ronalds, in 1834, measure up the Obelisk at Cado.

6 The tall stones of Brittany

Of the 6,192 standing stones, or menhirs, or peulvans to Breton archaeologists, which a count of 1880 reckoned to exist in France, 4,747 were located in Brittany, 3,450 of these being in Morbihan, the department containing Carnac. Many of these are over 20 feet tall, and some are even larger. These are often elegantly shaped with smoothed sides and tapering ends. Of such a type is that megalithic wonder, the *grand menhir brisé*, a pillar of stone almost 70 feet long, which now lies in four fragments on the spot where it once stood erect in the peninsula of Locmariaquer about six miles east of Carnac. The fifteen tallest menhirs in France, all of them in Brittany, were listed by Gabriel de Mortillet in 1885 with their approximate heights as follows:

Locmariaquer (Morbihan)	20.50 *metres or*	67.3 *feet*
Plésidy (Côtes-du-Nord)	11.12	36.5
Plouarzel (Finistère) at Kerloas	11.05	36.25
Louargat (Côtes-du-Nord)	10.30	33.8
Kérien (Côtes-du-Nord)	9.63	31.6
Dol (Ille-et-Vilaine) at Champ-Dolent	9.30	30.5
Plouarzel (Finistère) near the village	8.77	28.8
Pédernec (Côtes-du-Nord)	8.50	27.9
Glomel (Côtes-du-Nord)	8.50	27.9
Trégon (Côtes-du-Nord)	8.50	27.9
Scaër (Finistère)	8.33	27.3
Pleucadeuc (Morbihan) at la Grande-Brousse	8.00	26.25
Trégunc (Finistère)	8.00	26.25
Bégard (Côtes-du-Nord)	7.50	24.6
Carnihuel (Côtes-du-Nord)	7.50	24.6

The nearest British rival to these is the 29 ft. 8 in. (9 m) stone in the central trilithon at Stonehenge.

The *grand menhir brisé*, also called the fairies' stone, or *Mané er hroeh*, the stone of the grotto, in reference to the tumulus (now mostly destroyed for a car park) which lay at its foot, fell and broke into bits at an unknown date, probably between 1659 and 1722. The earlier date is that of an admiralty report on a local shipwreck, which mentioned that *la grande pierre de Locmariaker* was visible from the scene of the wreck. This, said Philippe Salmon in an article on the great stone (*L'Homme*, 10 April 1885) was a certain reference to the now fallen menhir, because that is the name by which it is still known and there is no other menhir so called. When Robien began his Carnac work in 1725 it was lying, as his drawing shows, in the same state as it is now, and he thought that it had fallen about three years earlier. He left no record or opinion of how the upset occurred. From the peculiar way in which the pieces are strewn, French experts last century proved by mathematical laws that a bolt of lightning was responsible, while the English professors, Thom and Atkinson, have proved by other mathematical laws that Le Rouzic was right in thinking it due to an earthquake. Professor Giot of Rennes has found records of a series of local earthquakes in AD 1286, but this discounts the 1659 report, and the questions of when and how the stone fell remain in the same state as all other important megalithic questions – still to be resolved.

The fragments of the *grand menhir brisé* are estimated to weigh together some 340 tons. It was stationed on high ground overlooking the sea, and the type of quartz-grained granite of which it is composed, which is also the material of the nearby ornate dolmen, the Table des Marchands, is not a local stone. The nearest quarry from which it could have come is at Pont-Aven in Finistère, over 50 miles from Locmariaquer and separated from it by ravines and deep sea inlets. This raises further questions about how the thing was done and what objects were served by such a vast labour. As Professor Thom puts it:

'One shrinks from making an estimate of how many man-hours were necessary [for quarrying, moving and setting up the stone]. We might guess that 20 men could work on each side cutting huge grooves, or rather valleys, into the rock leaving the stone to be eventually parted by the usual technique of cutting a row of slots, driving in dry wooden wedges and then pouring water on the wood. Atkinson has described how the Stonehenge menhirs were shaped by hammering the surface and removing the dust repeatedly. We can picture the men working until they had sunk a trench in the rock wide enough to work in and 10 or 12 feet deep. Then the stone had to be lifted and transported, inches at a time, using tree-trunks as levers – perhaps 40 levers lifting 8 tons each or perhaps lifting one end at a time. The fulcrums must have been of wood, but what bearing area of ground was needed for each? The organization and control of the labour force must have presented many problems, for example feeding and housing the men year after year. What was the urge behind it all and how were the labourers persuaded or forced to work?'

The most imponderable of the questions posed by the *grand menhir brisé* is that which asks why it was necessary to bring foreign rock to a spot where plenty of the local variety was available. Is there some property of that quartz granite which modern scientists have not identified or found a use for? The question is bound up with that of the original purpose of this and the other great menhirs, and though there are far from being any complete answers to that question, there are certain clues to aid its eventual solution.

Three different views of the same object: pieces of the great fallen menhir at Locmariaquer (Morbihan) drawn (*top*) by Blair and Ronalds in 1834 and by Léon Gaucheret about ten years later. *Below:* The earliest drawing of the great fallen menhir (*grand menhir brisé*) as seen by Robien in 1725.

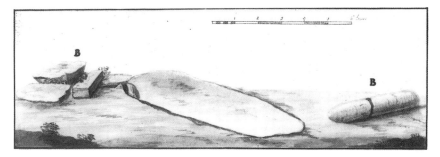

Three of the tall stones of Brittany drawn from early photographs. From left to right: the Giant of Kerdef near Carnac (Morbihan); the Menhir de Kerouezel at Porspoder (Finistère); the foot-shaped stone, about 23 feet tall, at Penmarch (Finistère).

The most obvious reason for erecting a tall pillar on high ground is to make it visible over long distances, and there are several features of the tall Brittany stones which seem to emphasize that function. Some of them are topped with crosses which have either been carved out of the stone or added onto it. There is no record of when most of these were done, but it has been suggested that the cross on top of a menhir may have replaced something else that once stood there, a fire basket containing a beacon light. One of the most interesting pieces of folklore that Cambry heard from an old sailor at Carnac was that 'each year in June the ancients added another stone to those already set up, and that all the stones were illuminated on the night before their ceremony'. The idea of a regular, ceremonial addition of a new stone to the alignments is supported by evidence of a similar practice in Pacific islands where surviving megalithic cults have been studied by anthropologists; and the belief that the stones were once lit up by fires has been expressed by archaeologists over many years. Alfred Watkins in *The Old Straight Track* described a menhir in Herefordshire, and others elsewhere, which showed signs of once having borne a beacon light. J. Bathurst Deane, the ally of Maudet de Penhouët and believer in ancient Egyptian serpent temples, gave reasons in an article (*Journal of the British Archaeological Association*, 1878) for thinking that the large menhirs in Brittany, many of which are near the sea, served as lighthouses, with fires on top of them

guarded by special attendants. He found places where pairs of them lined up
to point to dangerous offshore rocks. Lockyer in *Stonehenge*, writing about astronomical sightings from stone circles, claimed that 'some of the outstanding
stones must have been illuminated at night', and Alexander Thom, author of
the modern theory of megalithic astronomy, agrees with Lockyer on that
point.

Thom has offered a brilliantly worked out explanation for two features of
the *grand menhir brisé*: its position and its great height. These were both determined by the use of the great stone as a distant foresight, visible from megalithic observatories throughout the Carnac area as marking the extremes of the
moon's orbit. From prolonged study of megalithic remains in his native Scotland, Thom had shown that many such monuments were ideally situated and
designed to provide sightings and permanent records of lunar phenomena. In
the course of its complete cycle, which takes place over 18.61 years, the positions
of the rising and setting moon on the horizon vary between two extremes. This
makes the observation of the moon's complete range of movements more complicated and prolonged than in the case of the sun, which completes the return
journey between its two solstices in the course of a year. The moon's orbit is
further complicated by a slight, regular variation which is caused by the sun.
This variation together with the eight extreme lunar positions were found to

be recorded at many prehistoric sites by distant monuments, often sighted across wide stretches of sea. The extreme accuracy of the astronomical records which the megalith builders left spread out over their entire landscape shows that they possessed detailed knowledge of the moon's orbit and were thus in a position to predict the times of eclipses. Such advanced astronomical knowledge transcended the practical needs of ancient farmers and navigators, and it has been taken as evidence of a long succession of educated rulers in prehistoric northern Europe, similar to the Druids as detected by Stukeley and Cambry at megalithic sites, but even more ancient and wise than anyone had previously supposed.

Many of the tallest menhirs in Scotland had been found to mark the positions of ancient lunar observatories, and Thom was thus inclined to seek a lunar interpretation of the great stone at Locmariaquer. The results of his investigations were remarkable. The stone was found to be uniquely sited at the spot where some part of it, presumably lit up by a beacon fire, would have been visible against the rising or setting moon at the eight extreme positions achieved during its 18.61-year cycle, when viewed from eight distant observatories. Each pair of observatories had to be placed in alignment, one on either side of the great menhir and, for the sake of accuracy, several miles away from it. Thom was able to identify all these observatory positions, which in some cases still retained their megalithic sighting apparatus. From there most of the sighting lines towards the great menhir on the Locmariaquer peninsula passed over flat areas of water, allowing distant observation from the other headlands of Quiberon Bay, on which several of the observatories were sited, and in all cases the intervening ground and the horizons behind the menhir were low enough to give the observers a view of the moon behind an obelisk of the same height as that of the *grand menhir brisé*.

The task of finding the spot for a 'universal lunar foresight', capable of providing such a precise record of the moon's orbits as could the great menhir in its original state, has been estimated by Thom as comparable to that of engineering its transport and erection. These must have been preceded by astronomical researches over many generations, and Thom has recognized other sites in the Carnac area as relics of earlier lunar observatories which provided the information that eventually revealed the correct spot for the great universal foresight at Locmariaquer. Among the earlier stones is the menhir called the Giant of Manio, situated on a hilltop by the Carnac alignments, which could also have served as a foresight for the ancient moon watchers.

For years the Carnac archaeologists had concentrated on probing individual monuments with scarcely any thought that, apart from the stones in the alignments, they might be related to each other topographically, and so the effect on them of Thom's work has been rather stunning. In Lockyer's time at the turn of this century there had been several attempts at astronomical interpretations of some of the Breton monuments, notably by the French naval officer, Lieutenant (later Captain) Devoir, in Finistère, but the vast number of megalithic alignments to be chosen from in Brittany, and the occurrence of many for which there was no apparent astronomical explanation, was held against Devoir, and his work until lately had been as little regarded as had Lockyer's. Now the astronomical theory has come into its own, and there are those who think it capable of providing answers to all the problems bequeathed us by the megalith builders. Yet many features of megalithic sites cannot be thus explained, and they certainly had further uses than merely astronomical.

'Mound I', a painting by Richard Caston in 1974 of a landscape image
which constantly recurs to antiquarian travellers on 'the old straight
track': a tree-topped mound on the horizon.

The relationship between stone circles and seasonal paths and patterns of light, explored by the camera of John Glover at the Swinside stone circle, Cumbria.

Deane was surely right when he suggested that tall stones near the coast,
illuminated by night, would provide landmarks for ships, as some are known
to have done by day in modern times. There are also traditions that they
pointed the way across country to travellers or led up to churches, and several
old churches still preserve as relics the old fire baskets that once held the beacon light on their towers, perhaps in succession to megalithic beacon pillars
that once occupied their sites.

There are other traditions and customs associated with the tall Breton
stones which are so universal and old-established that they may well have
some bearing on aspects of their original purpose. Their shapes make them
natural symbols of the generative powers in nature, a symbolism which is
often explicit and accords with their legendary qualities as instruments of fertility. Denis Roche in his most entertaining of Carnac books (*Carnac*, 1969)
quotes from Georges Guénin's account of megalith folklore, *Pierres à légendes de
la Bretagne*, numerous instances of traditional practices intended to promote
fertility which are associated with Breton stones. From one of these it appears
that the *grand menhir brisé* was not just a possible lunar foresight but an actual
resort, annually on the first of May, for women in search of offspring, which
they hoped to achieve by bare-arsed slidings along its fragments. Mahé in
1825 recorded the Indecent Stone at Réguiny, which was so offensively shaped
that it was eventually 'cut down and made harmless'. The stone of St Renan at
Plouarzel, Finistère, the tallest at about 36 feet of all menhirs now standing,
has two protrudent knobs about four feet from the ground, and Fréminville
was the first to describe strange goings-on on the part of local couples there,
which were supposed by the man to bring his wife male children and by the
woman to make her the dominant partner in marriage. These practices were
reported by spies as late as 1917, by which time compulsory education and an
imposed alien culture had begun to show people how absurdly they had been
acting for so many centuries.

The megalithic construction programme, culturally related to the period of
settlement and the beginnings of agriculture, has traditional associations with
the fertility of the land and its inhabitants. Since this programme, and the
cults that derived from it, were continued over several thousand years, the
skills and labours of the megalith builders must surely have been of direct, ap-
preciable benefit to the lives of each generation. One observes, for instance,
that before the extinction of the megalith cults the land round Carnac was evidently more fertile than it is now, many areas having reverted from cultivated
fields to sandy wastes in quite recent times. That there were scientific principles behind the megalithic system has been proved by the archaeological astronomers, but neither they nor anyone else has yet produced a coherent explanation of the megalith phenomenon as a whole. Certain aspects of it hint at
mysteries which lie deeper than archaeologists are yet equipped to probe. The
French archaeologist, Charles Diot, who was also a *sourcier* or water-diviner,
published in 1935 a book called *Les Sourciers et les monuments mégalithiques*, in
which he showed with the assistance of the famous dowser, M. Merle, that
'every megalithic monument, without exception, was sited in relation to
underground streams, which abut them, or cross beneath them, or surround
them'. Recent researches in Britain have tended to confirm that statement,
but dowsers are notorious individualists and rarely agree on methods of proce-
dure; nor are they agreed on the nature of the radiations detected by their
rods. So the whole matter is still obscure. A confident assertion, however, is
that the great stones have yet many surprises for their future investigators.

Jorand fecit 1829.

Lith. de Engelmann

Opposite: The tall menhir which the builders of the cathedral at Le Mans, northern France, left standing outside the wall. There are other indications that the site was a prehistoric sanctuary and that the church there competed up to recent times with elements of an older faith. By 1829, when this drawing was made, the stone of Saint-Julien at Le Mans was becoming a curiosity for tourists.

Above: Menhirs cut into crosses at Cap Saint-Mathieu (Finistère).

Right: Also in Brittany, the tall stone with attached cross near Plonéour (Finistère).

91

Left: Two dolmens of Brittany. The Table des Marchands at Locmariaquer, known to an earlier generation of antiquarians as the Tomb of Caesar. The ornamented stone is one of the most famous examples of megalithic carving. In this mid-nineteenth-century illustration it has apparently become an ascetic's cell. The figures *below* are at a monument near Penmarch (Finistère).

Right: One of the finest of Breton menhirs, the religiously adorned stone of the Champ-Dolent, over thirty feet tall, near Dol (Ille-et-Vilaine). The name of its site, 'field of grief', is traditionally supposed to be derived from a bloody battle which took place there. Peace was restored when this stone plummeted down from heaven and stuck upright into the ground. It is also said that the stone is sinking at the rate of one inch every century, and that when it is entirely submerged the world will end. Early antiquarians identified it as a monument erected by Julius Caesar. The most remarkable theory about it was propounded by its owner to a visitor in 1779 (recorded in R.S. Kirby's *Wonderful Museum*, 1803). He stated: 'I have myself caused the earth to be removed round its base, to the distance of forty feet on every side; and I find that it joins to a prodigious rock, from which it seems to have sprung; so that I am induced to think, notwithstanding its name, that it may be a natural production.'

Below, right: A ruined dolmen shrine at Carnac forming the base of a cross.

93

Above: One of the tall stones of Carnac photographed early this century as a meeting place of the local gang.

Left: The great menhir of Kerloaz in Brittany, engraved from an early photograph in 1861.

Some menhirs of Africa and India. The two above are in Nigeria. That on the left is one of a group of five near the village of Oyengi in the land of the Nta. Each of the stones is called by the name of an ancestral chief, and their shape relates to their function as emblems of life and virility. On the right is the Yoruba chief, Akogun, who holds the office of Guardian to the tall stone called the Staff of Oranmiyan in Ife. The Staff, which had fallen, was restored some years ago.

Below: Monuments in the Khasi Hills, north of the Ganges in Assam. This district is crowded with megalithic structures which were being added to in modern times. It was once hoped that surviving megalithic cults in Asia would explain the prehistoric stones in Europe. The modern works, however, seem to be done out of respect for tribal custom, the original meanings of which are largely forgotten.

7 Stone Circles

The germ of 'megalithomania' which has developed into this book was implanted in its author about twenty years ago during a casual visit to a small, unimpressive stone circle standing on a featureless stretch of moorland in Derbyshire. While lingering about this dismal spot, he was surprised at the number of people who, for no obvious reasons, had also been impelled to visit it. It was as if something about the old stones or their site appealed instinctively to the imagination, while, for lack of any certain information, leaving the intellect unsatisfied. Further thoughts on the matter were aborted by a sudden rain storm which drove all parties back to their cars.

Later, a search of library shelves for archaeologists' explanations of stone circles had disappointing results. There were no modern books devoted exclusively to the subject, and in most works of prehistoric archaeology they received but brief and unenthusiastic mention. One author said that they were probably 'places of religious or other assembly'; others attributed to them an unknown 'ritual significance'. Excavations, it seemed, had been unrewarding in either treasure or information. The authorities had much to say about ancient burial sites and the objects and artefacts associated with them, but when it came to stone circles the eyes of the learned appeared to glaze over, as of men confronted with a mystery too familiar and insoluble to be of practical interest. The most to be learnt from them was that the old stones were not built or used by the Druids, not astronomically orientated, and definitely not related to each other or to other monuments by any system of design or arrangement. People who had suggested such things, their names including those of Stukeley, Lockyer and Watkins, were part of a ragged, discredited opposition, referred to by some professors as 'archaeology's lunatic fringe'.

And there on the same shelves, fringing the books of the modern authorities, were the actual works of those named heretics: Stukeley's magnificent volumes with their unsurpassed illustrations of Stonehenge, Avebury and other

Druid monuments; Lockyer's scholarly proofs of sun and star orientations in British stone circles; Watkins's *Old Straight Track* in which startling discoveries were set out in the gentle, unhectoring tone of a true antiquarian; and in all these writings could be sensed an enthusiasm for stone circles and allied subjects which seemed curiously lacking in the modern academic books.

Then there were books by people who had compiled or drawn conclusions from the universal traditions of megalithic monuments, often deriving these from an esoteric science and philosophy supposed to have existed in prehistoric antiquity: Wood-Martin's *Traces of the Elder Faiths in Ireland*, the works of Lewis Spence and Harold Bayley, Hadrian Allcroft's *The Circle and the Cross*, Dexter's *The Sacred Stone*, Beaumont's *Riddle of Prehistoric Britain*, the *Byways in Archaeology* and *Folk Memory* of Walter Johnson, Ignatius Donnelly on Atlantis, and – furthest out from the pale of scientific archaeology – the strange little books of J. Foster Forbes.

This nervous individual was of a Scottish landowning family in Aberdeenshire, one of their possessions being the stone circle near their castle at Rothiemay. There Forbes received early intimations of the powers of the old Druids and of how in their latter days they had misused these in black magic and bloody rituals. In his books from *The Unchronicled Past*, 1938, to *The Castle and Place of Rothiemay*, 1948, he outlined his views, that the Scottish circles dated from about 8,000 BC, that they were made by remnants of an Atlantean priesthood in efforts to restore order after their civilization had been shattered by cataclysm, and that they functioned both as lunar observatories and as receiving stations for the influences of the heavenly bodies at certain seasons. They were, he said, the instruments by which the pre-Celtic Druids, in their patriarchal phase, were able to control the earth's magnetism and uplift the entire people by integrating them with the elements of nature.

Well, maybe so, or perhaps not; but at least Forbes was a good trier, and some of his conclusions sound less outrageous to modern ears, conditioned by the new discoveries of the archaeological astronomers, than they did in his own time. They were mostly formed from the evidence of the 'psychometrist' ladies whom Forbes took around ancient sites in order to obtain their psychic readings of former events there. Also influential was Bishop Browne, whose book *Some Antiquities in the Neighbourhood of Dunecht*, commissioned by Lord Cowdray in 1921, included a picture of a cup-marked stone in the Rothiemay circle which he interpreted as a star chart, done in reverse image so that prints could be taken from it, about 6,000 years ago.

Unfortunately, Forbes did not live to see the great upsurge of megalithomania which began in the second half of the 1960s and welled up in earnest with the publication of Alexander Thom's *Megalithic Sites in Britain* in 1967. Professor Thom comes into almost every chapter of this book; indeed it is scarcely possible today to write or talk about stone circles without bringing in his name. His work at megalithic sites was seriously started only after his retirement from Oxford, where he was Professor of Engineering. Since that time he has by unaided effort revolutionized megalithic studies and illuminated prehistoric science and society to a degree which scarcely anyone had previously believed possible. Nobel Prizes, and certainly peerages, have been given for much less.

There are over 900 stone circles known in the British Isles. Many of these are now too wrecked to give information about their original dimensions, but of those more intact Professor Thom has visited and surveyed the majority. Analysis of the surveys has established that they form either true or geometrically flattened circles in a limited range of types, and that the unit of measure of their designers was the 'megalithic yard' of 2.72 feet. The same unit and the same canon of megalithic geometry occur in stone circles from the Orkneys and Western Isles to the tip of Cornwall and over into Brittany, thus implying the existence of a central scientific authority in prehistoric northern Europe and a similarity of purpose behind all stone circles and associated monuments. That purpose, according to Thom, was basically astronomical. Sighting lines were ranged from a point in the circle towards the sun at the solstices, equinoxes and the other feast days of the calendar, marked on the horizon by stone pillars or cairns or by natural features such as peaks, notches in mountain ranges or distant islands. Other lines indicated the transit of stars or of the moon, and Thom in his later work has emphasized the importance of lunar observation to the builders of the circles and the extreme accuracy they achieved in measuring the moon's complicated cycles. A remarkable feature of some sites – Castle Rigg, the stone circle in Cumberland, for example – is that the construction lines in the internal geometry of the design are also, when projected outwards from the circle, long-distance sighting lines towards astronomical events. The most finished example of this type of synthesis is Stonehenge, which has been sited in such a way that the formal geometry of the stone circles allows for twelve sighting lines, four to the extreme yearly positions of sunrise and sunset and eight to the turning points of the moon over its 18.61-year cycle. To find the required sites where the construction lines of a given geometrical design also form astronomical sighting lines represents a feat of surveying which could hardly be reproduced by modern methods.

The experience that inspired Thom to undertake his megalithic researches was in 1934 when he was sailing a yacht off the Atlantic coast of Lewis in the Outer Hebrides. One evening, while sheltering from a storm in an inlet called Loch Roag, he watched the moon rising, and silhouetted by its disc he saw a group of standing stones. It was Callanish, the circle of tall stones approached by five lines of menhirs, which M. Martin had described and figured in his book of 1703, *A Description of the Western Islands of Scotland*, where he called it a Heathen temple. Thom made a landing and approached the temple by way of an outcrop of rock lying on the extension of one of the stone alignments. From there the line of stones ran to a tall pillar near the centre of the stone ring, and above the pillar hung the pole star. The line of stones was pointing due north, exactly on the meridian. 'But there was no pole star in megalithic times,' wrote Thom. 'How was it done? From that minute I knew I had to deal with a highly developed culture, and everything I have uncovered since lends support to that.'

Thom's was by no means the first attribution of stone circles to ancient astronomers. A.L. Lewis in the 1880s, followed by Sir J. Norman Lockyer and Admiral Somerville, had found evidence linking megalithic sites to the heavenly bodies; but their theories had fallen foul of the archaeologists' objections that the stone circle builders were primitive, few in number and far more likely to have been concerned with survival than astronomy. These same objections were raised against Thom. One of his early papers, submitted to *Antiquity*, was returned with the editor's (O.G.S. Crawford's) comment scrawled across it: 'I do not believe your thesis.' In face of such prejudice, Thom realized that he would have to build up a solid case, statistically unassailable, if he was to get a hearing; and this over the years he proceeded to do, carrying his theodolite to stone circles in mountains and wildernesses for the careful surveys on which his conclusions were based.

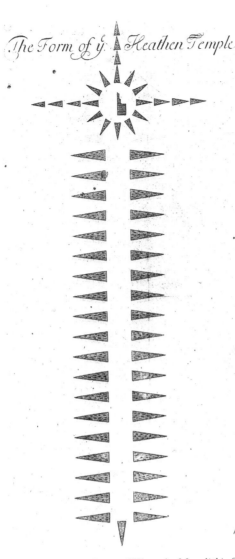

The Form of ye Heathen Temple

Scholarly attention was drawn to Callanish, the stone circle with an avenue and alignments in the Outer Hebrides, by Martin Martin in 1703. His plan of the stones has little to recommend it other than that it was the first published, but he recorded an interesting local tradition, that Callanish was 'a place appointed for worship in the time of Heathenism, and that the Chief Druid or Priest stood near the big Stone in the centre, from whence he address'd himself to the people that surrounded him'. This apparent survival of a tradition associating Druids with megalithic sites was found significant by the antiquarians of Stukeley's time. An earlier account of Callanish, by John Morisone in about 1680, made no mention of Druids, but told of a 'great enchanter' who had turned men to stone.

One of the effects of Thom's *Megalithic Sites* was that within a few years after its publication it was no longer possible to complain about the scarcity of literature on stone circles and theories prompted by them. Thom's revelation that prehistoric surveyors laid out straight, astronomical lines over many miles of country re-energized the few remaining members of the Old Straight Track Club whose founder, Alfred Watkins, had said much the same thing almost fifty years earlier. The Club's records, excavated from the vaults below Hereford Museum, were again consulted, the *Ley Hunter* magazine resumed publication, and there soon sprung up a crop of books by the ley hunters themselves. The first of these, like Anthony Roberts's *Atlantean Traditions in Ancient Britain*, 1970, were published by their authors, but ley hunter publishers, such as Michael Balfour of Garnstone Press, were quick to recognize the demand for such books, and the larger publishers followed with, among others, Paul Screeton's *Quicksilver Heritage*, 1974, and *The Ley Hunter's Companion*, 1977, by Paul Devereux and Ian Thomson.

The ley hunters' books introduced a startling new element into megalithic studies. From Watkins's observation that stone circles stood on straight lines, or leys, with other ancient sites, was developed the idea that the circles were centres of a natural telluric energy, and the alignments on which they stood were the paths of its seasonal transmission. One of the grounds for this theory was the repeated assertion by archaeological dowsers that their rods or pendulums detected strong radiations from stone circles and other spots of traditional sanctity, and also from certain tracks leading up to them.

The same idea has often been expressed by artists, as in the dolmen painting by 'A.E.' on page 60, and it is reflected in the association of megalithic sites with apparitions, weird happenings and ancient magical rites. It had also become evident, from Thom's discovery of so many permanent, elaborately constructed 'observatory' sites, often quite close together, that all this apparatus was far more complicated and refined than could be needed for practical purposes, such as providing a calendar for simple farmers and herdsmen.

In all the legends and physical relics of the megalith builders there are hints of an ancient system of ritual magic. Astronomy has always been closely associated with astrology, and in the relationships between megalithic monuments and the rays of the heavenly bodies at certain seasons there is a suggestion of alchemical processes at work, involving the marriage of cosmic forces with the vital energies of the earth. The geometrical forms and the symbolic numerology in the groundplans of stone circles are also those of traditional magic. Thus the consensus of ley hunters' opinions is that stone circles were used in connection with an elemental science, involving natural energies which may or may not be recognized today, whose purpose was to stimulate the fertility of the earth and its creatures, to promote prophecy or communication with the gods, and to regulate human affairs in accordance with the patterns in the heavens, as recommended in Plato's *Republic*.

The above picture of prehistoric antiquity has obvious roots in the ideas of Stukeley and the schools of Druidolatry that succeeded him. It represents the 'high' view of the past, in contrast to the rival 'low' view, whose classical expression is Thomas Hobbes's description of primitive life with:

'... no Culture of the Earth; no Navigation, nor use of the commodities that may be imported by Sea; no commodious Building; no Instruments of moving, and removing such things as require much force; no Knowledge of the face of the Earth; no account of Time; no Arts; no Letters; no Society; and which is worst of all, continuall feare, and danger of violent death; and the life of man solitary, poore, nasty, brutish, and short.'

Throughout the periodic ups and downs of megalithomania in the last three centuries, there have always been advocates of the Hobbesian, which was also the Darwinian, belief that prehistoric human life was savage and animal-like, with civilization as a unique invention of our own times. That view still has its representatives among archaeological writers, one of whom, Aubrey Burl, has made a notable contribution to the literature on stone circles with books including *The Stone Circles of the British Isles*, 1976, and *Rings of Stone*, 1979. In the latter, which is magnificently illustrated with Edward Piper's photographs, Burl comes out strongly against the ideas of the ley hunters and belittles the astronomical significance of stone circles. All these monuments, he suggests, were built by 'fanatical peasants ... zealous and primitive' who were 'driven by megalomania' to set up great stones as comforts to their disorientated lives. The circles were sometimes used as market-places by travelling stone axe dealers, but more usually as places of sacrifice, cremation and burial.

He points to the fact that in several cases of circles surrounding a tall pillar, as at Boscawen-un, that pillar is not placed at the exact centre of the ring. The reason for this was to allow sacrifices to take place at the centre and at the foot of the stone. The relics of the megalith builders, as interpreted by Burl, reveal their existences as 'savage, harsh and short, ridden with fears ...' and made further wretched by constant illness – a close paraphrase of Hobbes. Some circles, like Stonehenge, may have been astronomically orientated, but the idea behind this was symbolic, in relation to the cult of the dead. Stonehenge was designed principally for state funerals, although the carved axe-heads discovered on its pillars show that it was also used for primitive arms-dealing.

Oddly enough, for all the scorn he professes for the wretched megalith builders, Burl is still fascinated by their works. His books are informative and passionate, and although his theories have little bearing on the megalithic problem as redefined through the discoveries of modern researchers, they provide yet another illustration of the power of megalithomania on the imaginations of those afflicted by it.

With the physical evidence of the purpose of stone circles giving rise to so many totally diverse theories, the one source of information that remains constant and coherent is the folklore record. In the universal legends of megalithic sites the stones are alive and active, particularly at certain seasons, when they move of their own accord, dance in a ring, have powers of healing and fertility and bring ill luck to people who violate them. The most interesting body of oral traditions is that of Callanish, as summarized in O.F. Swire's *The Outer Hebrides and their Legends*, 1966. Besides the usual 'petrification' legend, representing the stones as the pagan elders of the district petrified by St Kieran, the remarkable story was told that the stones were brought there by a king who arrived in a large fleet with a retinue of priests and Africans. The Africans set up the stones, those who died in the process being buried within the circle. When the king departed he left behind the high priest and others, and they invited local people to assist in their rituals: 'The priests wore robes made of skins and feathers of birds, that of the Chief Priest being white with a girdle made from the neck feathers of mallard drakes; the other priests wore feather cloaks of mixed colours. The Chief Priest never appeared without wrens (or a wren) flying near him.'

Even more remarkable is an incident, also recorded by Miss Swire, which hints at the survival into modern times of pagan ceremonies at the Callanish stones and the strange effect produced by them.

'My mother, as a girl in the last half of the nineteenth century, used to visit Stornoway occasionally, staying with the Mathesons. One year she was there in June and there were also staying at the Castle other visitors, including an elderly member of the Scottish Society of Antiquaries. He had come in the hope of seeing some Midsummer Day customs at the Stones. He told the house party that as a boy he had spent several holidays in Lewis and had got to know the crofters with whom he stayed very well and, through them, many other families. He had learnt, he said, that the old people still held certain families in special respect and esteem as "belonging to the Stones", though quite how or why he did not know. Also, one old man had told him he could remember that when he was a child people visited the Stones secretly, especially at Midsummer and on May Day. The old man's parents had told him that when they were young the people went openly to the Circle but that the Ministers had forbidden all that, so now they went in secret, for it would not do to neglect the

This interesting record of the stones at Callanish, from a drawing by Colonel Sir Henry James in 1866, shows the horizontal divisions of the stones into weathered and light areas which resulted from the removal of peat from the site in 1857. The owner, Sir James Matheson, had five or six feet of the turf excavated and carted away, revealing the impressive size and other features of the monument. James's inspection of the site convinced him that tradition was correct in calling it a temple of the Druids, and he found it 'admirably adapted, both by its position and construction, to produce the greatest possible effect on a vast concourse of people, assembled to witness their dreadful sacrifices'.

Stones. The Antiquarian said that this old man had also told him that when the sun rose on Midsummer morning "Something" came to the Stones, walking down the great avenue heralded by the cuckoo's call. He had described the "Something" by a word, always the same word, which the boy did not know but he wrote it down as well as he could from the sound and later, being curious, showed it to a Celtic scholar of repute, who, in turn, showed it to various colleagues. They all agreed that it appeared to be an archaic word, probably pre-Gaelic and from a root common to all the British group of languages. It meant, they thought, the Shining, or Pure, or White one – Good, in fact, as opposed to dark, murky Evil – and probably had once been the epithet of a god. The Antiquarian himself thought it signified the Celtic sun-god Lugh. But Lugh belongs primarily to Ireland and the Irish gods and goddesses play little, if any, part in Hebridean lore, anyhow by name.'

Here is an explicit account of the sort of happening which may have occurred at stone circles at the seasonal festivals. In ancient accounts of pagan ceremonies it is emphasized that the invoked god made an actual appearance

I Kip Sculp

The Rollright stones in Oxfordshire were a popular subject to early antiquarian artists. This view of the circle and outlying stones was engraved by Kip for the seventeenth-century *Britannia* of Camden, and another drawing was published by David Loggan in 1677. In the same period John Aubrey made drawings of Rollright for his *Monumenta Britannica*.

before the assembled people. However explained, that was certainly the effect produced. Some of the older religions, as Shintoism in Japan, preserve forms of geomancy by which naturally sacred spots are discovered and gods induced to inhabit them.

In pondering the meaning and methods behind these practices, one is inclined to wonder about the natural characteristics that distinguish a sacred spot, and about the events or illusions that might be created there at the climax of a sunrise ceremony before an excited assembly. An aspect of the problem is now under investigation through the 'Dragon Project', sponsored by the *Ley Hunter* journal, at the Rollright stone circle in Oxfordshire, where sensitive instruments are used to measure the intensity of the energy fields around the stones and the variations produced in them at sunrise in various seasons. The theory to be tested in this novel development of megalithomania is that stone circles were erected at sites where, under certain astronomical conditions, a source of natural energy would be generated, for which the ancient priests found a practical use to the benefit of themselves or the people.

Whatever the results, this type of investigation is certainly more imaginative and a great deal less destructive than the excavations to which so many circles have been subjected – at the gain of next to nothing in the way of information about their meaning. The intervention of astronomers, ley hunters, dowsers, neo-Druids and men with scientific instruments has, as it were, thrown the stone circles open to the public, thus generating far more interest in studying them and protecting them than has been the case when they have been the exclusive preserve of archaeologists.

Two stone circles near Avebury drawn by William Stukeley in 1723: the 'Celtic Temple' at Winterborne and (*above*) part of the Sanctuary which was destroyed soon after Stukeley made his drawings of it. In the background are Silbury Hill and the West Kennet avenue of stones which ran in a curve from Avebury to the Sanctuary. Stukeley took the avenue to represent the body of a serpent whose head was formed by the Sanctuary's two concentric circles. In his later drawings he was unable to resist the temptation to make the circles more like a snake's head by representing them as ovals.

Below: A nineteenth-century view from the ruined dolmen called The Whispering Knights to the circle of Rollright Stones, the Oxfordshire monument which has recently been a favourite testing ground of theories and experiments on the nature of the megalithic science.

Right: Monuments on Dartmoor engraved from mid-nineteenth-century drawings by C.F. Williams of Exeter for Samuel Rowe's *Dartmoor.* The stone avenue (*above*), on the North Teign, was one of those pointed out by J. Bathurst Deane and other followers of Stukeley's theory of dracontia as an obvious serpent image. Rowe described the 'sacred circle' at Scorhill (*below*) as 'by far the finest example of the rude but venerable shrines of Druidical worship in Devonshire'. Similar impressions are received by modern visitors to this strange, lonely site. It is one of the places where the sort of weird events which contribute to modern megalithic folklore are most frequently located. Tales are told of engines and instruments which failed in its vicinity, and local riders find that their horses are unwilling to approach it. R.E. St Leger-Gordon, who records the latter inhibition in her *Witch-craft and Folklore of Dartmoor,* 1965, also notes that the circle has 'acquired the reputation of being in some way eerie'.

Left: Castle Rigg circle near Keswick in the Lake District, a handsome illustration from J.B. Pyne's *Lake Scenery of England*, 1859. Long one of the most popular of stone circles for its completeness and the beauty of its site, Castle Rigg has intrigued modern researchers because of the subtle relationships between the arrangement of its stones, the landmarks in the mountains surrounding it, and the seasonal positions of the heavenly bodies.

Above: A detail of Gibb's 1862 prospect of megalithic monuments in the neighbourhood of Maeshowe in Orkney. The great chambered mound of Maeshowe is in the foreground; behind it to the right is the Brogar, and, on the left, the Watchstone.

Left: Among the thousands of illustrations of English scenery and monuments made by Samuel Hieronymus Grimm are some fine drawings of megalithic antiquities in Somerset and Wiltshire. This detailed view of Stanton Drew, dated August 1789, is of comparable quality and interest to Stukeley's drawing (page 16) of the circles.

Sainte Geneviève with her flock in a stone circle, painted in the late
sixteenth century. This picture, belonging to the Church of Saint-Merri in
Paris, is one of the earliest and most interesting of megalithic illustrations.
Accounts of its subject and history are to be found in *Antiquity*, XLVII and
XLVIII. The fifth-century shepherdess, Sainte Geneviève, patron saint of
Paris, lived outside the city, at Nanterre, where relics of a stone circle were
to be seen at the beginning of this century. It had probably been destroyed
at or shortly after the time of the Revolution. Sainte Geneviève saved Paris
from Attila's Huns by the power of her prayers, and the circle which she
frequented was said to have a similar power over the River Seine, repelling
its waters in times of flood.

8 Megalithomania at the Land's End

One of the magnetic areas of England is its extreme western tip, the high, rocky Land's End peninsula of Cornwall. Since the middle of last century when the railway reached Penzance, the area has been colonized by painters, attracted by its clear light and other qualities, which were evidently appreciated in far earlier ages. Celtic saints built their oratories among its rocks, and its unique collection of megalithic sites shows an active population in prehistoric times. On account of these, the Land's End district has become a classic field of antiquarianism, where many of the classic controversies that enliven it have had their origin.

In 1754 the Rev. Dr William Borlase, Rector of Ludgvan, a village near Penzance, published his *Antiquities of Cornwall,* in which for the first time were described and figured many of the stone circles, menhirs and cromlechs for which the district was thus made famous. With these were other types of monuments such as are no longer featured in archaeological works: logan or rocking stones, rock idols and rock basins. Borlase was one of an old-established, numerous local family, he knew the district and many of its people intimately, and at Ludgvan, where he lived and ministered for fifty years until his death in 1772, he had leisure enough to pursue local studies. These were in fact the only occupation available to him, for his parish was far removed from libraries and learned company, and he had no interest in the sports and hunts which took up the time of his neighbours. His *Antiquities* and *Natural History of Cornwall* (1758) are monuments to a lifetime of first-hand enquiry into every aspect of his native county, and his other book, on the Islands of Scilly, was praised by Dr Johnson as 'one of the most pleasing and elegant pieces of local enquiry that our country has produced'. He corresponded with the notable scholars of his time, including Pope and Stukeley, and it was to him that Stukeley turned for information on the Cornish relics of the ancient Druids.

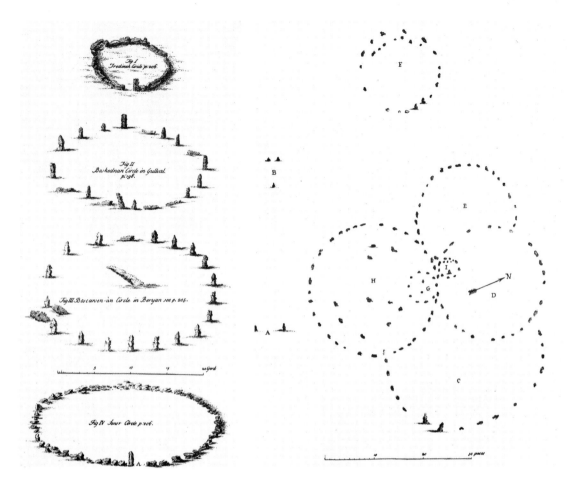

Fig I Fredmen Circle p.206.

Fig II Boskednan Circle in Gulval. p.198.

Fig III Boscawen-ün Circle in Beryan see p. 205.

Fig IV Sınor Circle p.206.

Two of the stone circles in west Cornwall, figured by Dr William Borlase in 1754, and (right) his mysterious plan of a group of intersecting circles in the same district, at St Just. The stones of this group were long ago removed, for building purposes it is said, and their original site is no longer known.

Of these Borlase had recognized many examples. Western Cornwall had evidently been one of the spots which the Druids particularly favoured: its stone circles were their temples, the outlying single stones their idols, and their notables were buried beneath the capstones of its cromlechs or quoits. At every curious rock formation, tor and rocking stone he saw the judgment seats of the Druids and their places of augury and sacrifice. These sites could in many cases be identified by the basins and channels which the Druids had cut into the rock to serve as holy water stoups for the purifications which preceded their usually bloody rituals.

Stukeley was delighted by the relics of Druidism thus revealed in the far west, but it became apparent that he and Borlase differed in their interpretation of them. For Stukeley, Druidism was the font of true religion, and he found nothing but virtue in the ways of the old priesthood; but Borlase was in two minds about them. On the one hand, he agreed with Caesar and the other classical authorities that the Druids were masters of astronomy, natural medicine and other sciences, that their philosophy was learned and noble, and that they kept order, upheld the peace and gave judgments as well as could be expected of people who lived in times before Christ's redemption. On the other hand, they undoubtedly practised human sacrifice, and in their latter days they had fallen into the error of acknowledging many gods instead of One, which had caused them to worship idols. A proof of this was the number of rock idols in the form of stone pillars and outcrops, sometimes shaped by the Druids and sometimes natural, to be found all over the Cornish moors. Their different shapes revealed the particular god that each was intended to represent. Also, the Druids practised magic, and that was something Borlase could not approve of. In a letter written in 1728, which is now kept in the Penzance Library, he had reproved a man of St Ives whom he suspected of conjuring, trafficking with the devil and divining for lost property, warning him of the dangers in such proceedings. Such rustic curiosities and other customs, still alive in his time, as torchlight processions and seasonal bonfires on hilltops, were recognized by Borlase as survivals from the days of Druid magic. Yet, like many other pious witch-hunters, Borlase could never make up his mind about the efficacy of magic, whether ancient or modern. As a clergyman, he accepted the Bible's authority for the existence of active, though evil forces behind it; but his education assured him that it was all mere conjuring and deception. The Druids, he declared, owed their position to their reputation as magicians, and this they supported by their various arts and 'lucrative juggles' around their rocking stones.

It came as a blow to Stukeley that his promising colleague in the study of Druids should take such a low-minded view as to suppose them guilty of idolatry. By the time *Antiquities of Cornwall* appeared in print, he was no longer corresponding with Borlase, and the two Druid theorists were never reconciled. Borlase's critical view of the Druids, which he had derived at least in part from study of their monuments, appealed to scholars as more likely and more comprehensible than Stukeley's version. Other examples of Druid rock idols were identified about the country, notably by Major Rooke in Yorkshire, and Druid thrones and oracles revealed themselves in the rocky wildernesses and even at stone circles. The 'cove' at Stanton Drew was supposed in 1821 'to have been erected for judicial purposes, where the Druids sat and administered justice to the neighbouring tribe'. At stone circles were also found the relics of human sacrifice which Borlase had observed near the Merry Maidens circle in west Cornwall – stones with holes drilled through them. These, he had suggested, were used to secure the Druids' victims before their moment came to feature in the ceremonies, and a hundred years later an illustration of a stone circle in Yorkshire, including a stone with holes through it, showed exactly how the thing might have been done (see page 134).

A typical landscape in the west of England at the time of the Druids, from Dr Borlase's *Antiquities of Cornwall* (1754).

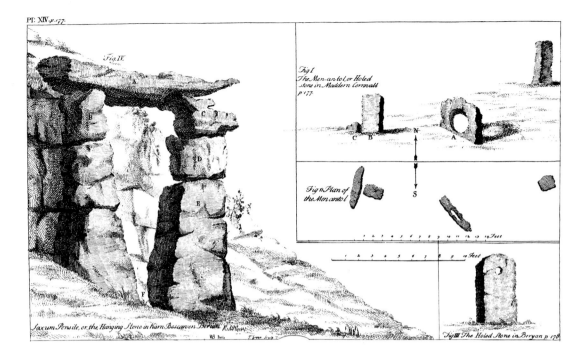

Fig. IV.

Saxum Pensile, or the Hanging Stone in Karn Boscawen Berean. p. 180.

Fig I
The Men-an-tol or Holed
stone in Maddern Cornwall
p 177.

Fig II Plan of
the Men an tol

Fig III The Holed Stone in Berryan p 178

The ancient pillars and stone ring called Men-an-tol in west Cornwall, carefully recorded by Dr Borlase.

Even in Borlase's time the quiet war between English and French scholars about whose monuments were the older was already going strong. The French were jealous of Stukeley's Druids, with their famous temples of Stonehenge and Avebury and their claim to be the original patriarchs of true religion. Voices had been heard from across the Channel urging the greater antiquity of the French Druids and their monuments. On that point Dr Borlase was firm. Caesar had stated clearly that Druidism had first arisen in Britain and later passed over to France. It had to be admitted that the first people to arrive in England had come by way of Gaul, but it was they who had invented Druidism, which was native to Britain alone, and the British Druids and Druid monuments were therefore earlier than those of the French. He concluded: 'France would not willingly be indebted to her neighbours in a point of such consequence and antiquity; but this humour of hers will not deprive so great an author as Caesar of the weight, which he must always have with unprejudiced readers, till she can produce testimonies of equal, or superior authority to refute him.'

It was a challenge which Cambry, as described in a previous chapter, was later to take up in most spirited fashion on behalf of Carnac and the Emperor Napoleon.

The new railway that brought the Victorian artists down to the Land's End district also brought the archaeologists. One of the first to arrive, in 1860, was a brilliant antiquarian, James Orchard Halliwell, whose checkered career had included his election as a fellow of the Royal Society at the age of eighteen, accusations against him of being a manuscript thief, and his marriage to the daughter and heiress of Sir Thomas Phillips, one of the most fanatical book collectors of all times. It was Borlase's *Antiquities* that had attracted Halliwell to the Land's End. 'I had never opened that singular and valuable folio volume', he wrote, 'without feeling a curiosity and desire to examine the original monuments there described, and to pay a visit to a land which the uncornish reader of that work pictures to himself as literally strewn with solemn cromlechs and hoary circles, all popularly known as memorials of the giants of old.'

During his stay at Penzance, Halliwell visited the monuments described by Borlase, and in his *Rambles in Western Cornwall by the Footsteps of the Giants*, 1861, he made the first record of several others. He also met an impoverished young local scholar, John Thomas Blight, son of a Penzance schoolmaster, who was already immersed in the work of his short, tragic lifetime, trying unsuccessfully to make a living as a professional archaeologist and antiquarian illustrator. He was a perfect guide to the antiquities of the Land's End district, having drawn and engraved many of them to illustrate his two volumes on Cornish stone crosses and his popular book for tourists, *A Week at the Land's End*. Blight's early patron had been the famous Vicar of Morwenstowe in north Cornwall, the Rev. R.S. Hawker, the opium-eating poet and a mystic in the tradition of the old Celtic saints. Hawker was also extremely irascible, and he quarrelled with Blight, who was thus on the look-out for new means of gaining introductions to the important men in the world of antiquarianism who might advance his career. These Halliwell promised to supply. He was then in the process of making himself the leading authority on the life and works of Shakespeare, and he engaged Blight to make drawings in the neighbourhood of Stratford-upon-Avon of every building and monument that Shakespeare himself could possibly have seen. Through this and other archaeological commissions Blight was able to study prehistoric monuments beyond Cornwall. Throughout the 1860s his accurate, finely engraved views of megalithic sites illustrated his own and other people's articles in the archaeological journals. In 1870 he began a book, *The Cromlechs of Cornwall*, with which he intended to surpass Borlase's *Antiquities*. But he ended as another victim of Borlase's Druids. Only by hard, incessant labours had he been able to afford to continue in a profession whose other members were mostly gentlemen of independent means. The pressure on his brain became too great and delusions set in. He announced to Penzance that the Druids had returned in the guise of Church of England clergymen and were preparing to restore their bloody rites by the stone idols. *The Cromlechs of Cornwall* became incoherent; the printer refused to proceed further, and Blight was taken to the County Lunatic Asylum at Bodmin. Some years later, his publisher informed readers of a new edition of Blight's *Churches of West Cornwall* that its author was dead. In fact, unknown to all but a few, he lingered on at the Asylum for forty years until his actual death in 1911.

The Men-an-tol in 1856 by J.T. Blight. In the interval since Borlase drew the monument in the previous century the stones appear to have been moved in line with each other. The use of the holed stone for divination and for curing sickly infants continued into modern times.

Chun Quoit in west
Cornwall, by W.C.
Borlase, 1871.

Blight's papers passed into the hands of his colleague, another native Penzance archaeologist, William Copeland Borlase, a great-great-grandson of the old Doctor, who used them, together with his ancestor's manuscript notes, to complete his *Naenia Cornubiae*, published in 1872. In this the new Borlase utterly banished the Druids from the rocks and monuments assigned to them in the *Antiquities of Cornwall*. They were, he said, mere 'hoary phantoms', dreamed up by his great-great-grandfather and other imaginative people of his time, whose influence was solely responsible for the popular traditions which associated Druids with prehistoric sites. Modern researchers had been unable to show that any of these traditions were in existence before the publication of old Dr Borlase's *Antiquities,* while modern science had proved that megalithic monuments were mostly sepulchral, 'and therefore presumably unconnected with any distinct religious observances'. In the family tradition, Borlase had strong views on Druids. His attitude to them was of hatred and scorn, strengthened perhaps by their effect on poor Blight. Their arts he described as 'miserable', their ceremonies as 'revolting'. His book is recognized as a pioneer work of 'scientific' archaeology.

W.C. Borlase's writing is most valuable as a record of Cornish megalithic sites, but most of his science consisted in digging into them and around them in search of the funerary objects that supported the sepulchral theory. Thus he assisted in the destruction of monuments which he deplored when it was done by other people. Out of the many thousands of barrows in Cornwall, he wrote, 'more than one half have been opened, as a mere matter of curiosity, by persons leaving no record whatever of the result'. Borlase made careful notes of his finds, but his rifling of so many sites – far beyond the point where any new sort of information could be gained from them – has been regretted by later archaeologists. In his time, ancient sites were under attack as never before by farmers reclaiming waste lands and by the vast mining operations throughout Cornwall. Monuments were disappearing daily, Borlase noted; and the same destructive processes have continued in force up to the present. Of the 34 standing stones described in 1974 in the author's *The Old Stones of Land's End,* two had been removed from their sites by the time the new edition came out in 1979. Even in western Cornwall, one of the most deeply studied archaeological areas of Britain, it is still only the more famous monuments that are safe from anyone's whim to destroy them.

To make up for the damage done by his spade there are Borlase's meticulous notes and drawings of Cornish sites and his wonderful work of scholarship, *Dolmens of Ireland*, 1897. Like Blight, he guided many learned visitors to the antiquities of the Land's End district, and with one of them, the Rev. W.C. Lukis, he collaborated to produce the folio volume, *Prehistoric Stone Monuments: Cornwall*, which was intended as the first of a series containing Lukis's plans of British prehistoric monuments. In fact it was the only volume to appear, the rest of the material being destroyed in a fire at the printer's.

A great deal has been written about the impressive collection of ancient sites at the Land's End, and in 1971 the area gained further distinction. Vivien Russell's *West Penwith Survey*, published that year, provided a complete list of all known sites within the fourteen parishes that make up the Land's End peninsula, together with references to every mention of them in the literature.

One of the subterranean structures called 'fogous', characteristic of west Cornwall, which have been identified by the guesses of different authorities as dwellings, refuges, storage pits, hermitages and initiation chambers. This example, the 'cave' at Carn Euny, is represented in nineteenth-century drawings by J.T. Blight (*above*) and W.C. Lukis.

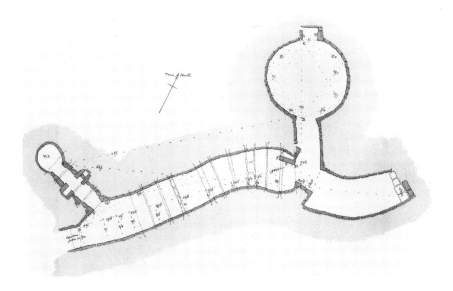

This was the first time such a work had ever been done. Miss Russell spent many years in libraries and in the field before completing it, and her achievement has proved of great value, particularly to a strange group of people who were beginning from the middle of the 1970s to interest themselves in the antiquities of the Land's End – the statisticians.

These people had had dealings with Cornish archaeology on a previous occasion. At the beginning of this century, Sir J. Norman Lockyer had been active in the Land's End district, investigating the astronomical properties of its stone circles. He had formed a local society to encourage these studies. Lord Falmouth, who owned many of the sites, was its first president. In 1907 they erected a hut within the Tregeseal stone circle near St Just to shelter parties making observations of the sun and stars. Lockyer had identified landmarks behind which Arcturus and the Pleiades would have appeared in times ranging from 2330 to 1270 BC, and other marks for the solstitial and May Day sunrises. To Lockyer it all seemed very clear. The old Cornish Druids should be characterized not by their bloody sacrifices, but by their acuteness in astronomical observation. He published the results of his west Cornish surveys in the second edition of his *Stonehenge and Other British Monuments Astronomically Considered*. He was undone, however, by the statisticians. They pointed out the irregularity of Lockyer's proceedings. He had chosen a place of observation and then related marks and monuments visible from it to the positions of the heavenly bodies at various dates and seasons; but he had not noted how many other possible observatory sites there were or how many other possible marks; and he had referred to so many different dates, feast days and stars, both rising and setting, that almost any mark could be made to line up with some astronomical event at some time in the past. In vain Lockyer protested that the number of bright stars he reckoned with was very limited and that his results were something more than arbitrary. He had presented his data with no respect for the statisticians, and they ruled him out of court. He was purged from the records of Cornish archaeology, and even in Miss Russell's otherwise inclusive *Survey* there is no mention of his work at the Land's End. A recent guidebook to St Buryan, one of the Land's End parishes, states that the one thing known for certain about stone circles is that they are not astronomical.

Yet, on further inspection, some of Lockyer's astronomical sighting lines from stone circles have an interesting feature which he himself never seems to have noticed. Two of his lines from Boscawen-un circle and one from Tregeseal, if projected further eastward, pass over other megalithic sites. In one of the Boscawen-un examples, two more standing stones and the probable sites of two fallen ones, unrecorded by Lockyer or Miss Russell, were found on the extension of a line drawn by Lockyer between the circle and an outlier. Other alignments of three or more stones occur throughout the district, and in *The Old Stones of Land's End* some of these alignments were described together with the sites comprising them. The claim made was that the alignments were so accurate and repetitive that they looked like products of design rather than chance.

This claim was soon challenged by the archaeological statisticians, who recognized the small, isolated Land's End peninsula with its many prehistoric sites as the ideal testing ground for the whole question of leys or aligned sites, first raised by Alfred Watkins nearly sixty years previously. By use of a computer the total number of alignments can be discovered and then compared with the number that would be expected from a random distribution of sites. This experiment was first made by Hutton-Squire and Gadsby of *Undercurrents*

magazine, followed by Simon Broadbent and others, each using different
methods of defining and computing alignments. Dr Broadbent's paper, 'Sim-
ulating the Ley Hunter', was read to an assembly of ley hunters and statisticians at a meeting of the Royal Statistical Society in December 1979. Like his
predecessors', Broadbent's statistics showed a greater incidence of alignments
among the Land's End stones than might be accounted for by chance. He did
not however accept his own figures as proof that megalithic alignments existed. There were problems with statistical theories and data bases, and these became further complicated as the meeting proceeded by the arcane formulae
produced by other statisticians. One of them, Dr Hansford-Miller, warned his
colleagues that, according to tradition, the stones at megalithic sites were impossible to count. He himself had experienced that difficulty at the Rollright
stones, and it had made him very dubious of all megalithic researches which
depended on counting stones.

To their credit, most of the ley-hunting statisticians have not been content
to take their material solely from written sources, such as Miss Rusell's *Survey*,
but have tramped around the Land's End district to seek it it in the field. This
has led to the discovery of other stones to add to their data-bases, and at the
time this is being written they are still at their quest. Whatever their results,
their intervention has been valuable because it has drawn attention to the lesser monuments about the district, many of them still quite unprotected, which
may be as important as the more impressive sites as clues to the megalithic
riddle. It has also had the effect that several of the statisticians, having never
seen an old stone before, have become aware that there is more to the subject
than can be reckoned by computers. Visitors to megalithic sites often comment on the strange atmosphere or the strange feelings they have there, and
there are rumours that some of these sites are still resorted to by groups of
witches, pagans and occultists. The commonly held view in those circles is expressed in Ithell Colquhoun's book, *The Living Stones: Cornwall*, 1957, that the
tors and 'rock idols', worshipped by Dr Borlase's Druids, are 'the abraded
foundations of a power-house where Sarron and Samothes, royal colonists
from Atlantis, stored their subtle force', and that the Cornish stone circles are
still active as magnetic accumulators, 'repositories still of ancient power ... the
living stones'. Miss Colquhoun hints that these power sources are used not
only by modern pagans but by other groups who 'absorb this force and dis-
tribute it by Christian means'.

An archaeologist who was well aware of the unidentified power in the Cornish stone circles was the late T.C. Lethbridge. In *The Legend of the Sons of God*,
1973, he described a visit to the Merry Maidens circle and the attempt he and
his wife made to date it by use of a diviner's pendulum. The date of 2540 BC
was plausibly obtained for it, but in the course of their proceedings the Leth-
bridges were alarmed by the strong electric shocks they felt and by the sensation that the stones were rocking and dancing. 'But why did anybody wish to
store up electronic power in such places?' asked Lethbridge. The astronomical
theory seemed to him unconvincing, and his suggestion was that the circles
were built as guiding power-beacons for the space craft of the culture-bearing
extraterrestrials who from time to time visit this planet.

Whatever other powers they may possess, the old stones of western Cornwall have a demonstrable power to stimulate the imagination. No doubt they
will continue for many years to retain this power, and the range of theories by
which they have already been illuminated will be further extended in times to
come.

Opposite: This great rock, nobly depicted by Richard Tongue in 1835, was described and illustrated by Dr Borlase in 1757. He called it 'one vast egg-like stone, placed on the points of two natural rocks, so that a man may creep under the great one, and between its supporters'. It stood in the parish of Constantine in Cornwall, and was known as The Tolmen. Its length along its greater, north-south axis was, according to Borlase, thirty-three feet. The pits and channels carved into its upper surface indicated, he thought, its former use by the Druids. Despite its weight, which he estimated at 750 tons, he believed that the Druids might have erected it on its supporters; for 'the Ancients had powers of moving vast weights, of which we have now no idea'. The Tolmen was disgracefully destroyed by quarrymen in 1869.

The Druid legend spread widely, attaching itself to all manner of picturesque rock formations, and thus spicing their interest to tourists. Early in the nineteenth century Major Rooke contributed articles to *Archaeologia* on the Druidical rock idols of the north of England, supporting his conclusions with some persuasive illustrations. These (*above* and *below*) are of some of the Brimham Rocks in Yorkshire. *Below left:* Joseph Blight's woodcut of the famous rocking stone near the Land's End, referring to an earlier legend than that of Borlase's Druids: that the monumental Cornish rocks were raised by a race of giants.

An early excavation of human remains from a barrow near Stonehenge, illustrated in 1600. The castle in the background, which appears in most Stonehenge drawings from 1575 through the seventeenth century, has never been identified.

9   Excavators at Work

There is little evidence, in the pictorial record, that the great nineteenth-century barrow excavators ever did any work. For the most part they are depicted in attitudes of elegant supervision, often with picnic hampers and women-folk, while sturdy workmen, eager for the sight of buried treasure, shovel away the ancient monument. Even in the earliest of these illustrations, the view of Stonehenge by William Rogers in 1600, the men in the foreground digging up bones from a barrow are being directed by a gesticulating gallant.

The practice of despoiling the dead interred within mounds is almost as old as mound-building itself. Despite traditions of demons and ghostly guardians and of the ill fortune that pursues violators of ancient sanctuaries, there have always been fools who were prepared to take the risk. Examples of the dreadful things that have happened to such people are recorded throughout archaeological literature. Typical is J. T. Blight's remark in *A Week at the Land's End*, 1861: 'The person who pulled down this cromlêh [West Lanyon Quoit] is said to have brought a number of misfortunes about him in consequence; thus his cattle died and crops failed, which left a warning impression on the minds of his neighbours.'

Such warning impressions about the dangers in sacrilege helped to preserve megalithic sites everywhere for hundreds of years, long after their original or traditional uses had been forgotten. Most people have always been too frightened of the dead to attempt robbing them, and so it happened that antiquarians at the beginning of the nineteenth century found themselves heirs to a vast stock of unopened tumuli, which they fell upon in the manner here illustrated. Some were motivated by desire for loot, others by the spirit of scientific inquiry, or by the two combined; but whatever the motive for excavating a prehistoric mound the result is much the same. Even if the monument is not entirely removed in the course of archaeological excavation, as has often been

Portraits of Sir Richard Colt Hoare (1758-1838) and, *right*, William Cunnington (1754-1810). These two collaborated in opening up and despoiling most of the great prehistoric sites in Wessex.

the case, once its structure is broken it is open to erosion by the elements and will gradually disintegrate. The respectable savants of last century, who rode about the country opening barrows and removing their treasures, also removed the inhibitions which had previously deterred local people from doing likewise. Many important monuments have totally disappeared since their excavation, and so have many of their contents. Loss of prehistoric artefacts during or following their disinterment has taken place on a large scale. Those that passed into private collections have commonly been dispersed with no record of their histories, and losses through theft or fire or other accidents occur in even the best regulated museums.

At the beginning of the nineteenth century Sir Richard Colt Hoare and his chief excavator, William Cunnington, drilled into most of the great barrows on Salisbury Plain and accumulated the hoard of precious objects in gold, bronze, flint, stone and clay which formed the wonderful collection of antiquities, formerly kept at Hoare's mansion, Stourhead, and now in the Devizes Museum. Cunnington also helped with the compilation of Hoare's *Ancient Wiltshire*, completed in 1820 in two folio volumes with illustrations by Philip Crocker who was employed on Hoare's Stourhead estate as a surveyor and draughtsman. The credit due to Hoare for this magnificent work is tarnished by his selfishness in despoiling so many previously intact monuments out of curiosity or acquisitiveness. Edward Downman, author of an unpublished work, 'Earthworks in Wiltshire', written in 1908, put the charge against him in strong words (quoted here from Michael Balfour's *Stonehenge and its Mysteries*, 1979):

'Tumuli and Beacon Mounds were once the unique glory of Wiltshire, no other part of England being able to boast of so many: these had been respected for long ages both by the owners of the land, the farming classes, and the wise

The Fairy Knowe of Pendrich, Stirlingshire, one of many Scottish sites of that name which were associated with phantoms and weird events, undergoing excavation in 1860. Inside was a stone chamber containing a fine urn.

country folk, till in an evil day curious men and idle, such as R.C. Hoare (may his coffin be split into firewood and his monument be split up into paving stones), with no reverence for the resting places of the dead, or consideration for people yet to come, under the pretence of science and historical research, set to work to destroy these ancient tombs, or what they thought were ancient tombs; hence the ruin and wreck which meets the eye of the true antiquary. Where is the Norman Castle mound of Marden, the destruction of which Hoare commenced in AD 1809, mistaking in his ignorance a castle mound for one of the graves of the ancient folk, the contents of which he desired to ravish? where — ? But enough, my choler rises and my hand quivers as I write of these vandals who have disgraced the name of antiquary.'

The righteousness of Downman's choler is unaffected by his own belief that the earthworks of Wiltshire were of Norman construction.

The three main techniques of exploring ancient mounds, established in the early days of archaeology, were: to demolish them altogether, to cut slices out of them or, in Hoare's favourite fashion, to drill down into the centre from the top. The first of these methods was preferred by Lieutenant-General Pitt-Rivers (formerly Lane Fox; he changed his name on inheriting his estate), the acclaimed father of scientific archaeology. 'Having retired from active service on account of ill health, and being incapable of strong physical exercise, I determined to devote the remaining portion of my life chiefly to an examination of the antiquities on my own property,' he wrote at the beginning of his *Excavations in Cranborne Chase*, 1887.

Cranborne Chase was part of the large Pitt-Rivers estate in East Dorset. It was thick with ancient earthworks and it was archaeologically virgin territory. Its wooded, chalk uplands had been a hunting ground of King John, and it remained a deer park, guarded by keepers, until 1830 when it was disenfranchised and the deer destroyed. Large tracts had never been touched by the plough when General Pitt-Rivers came into possession of it. He archaeologized it ruthlessly. In his classic excavation of the long barrow called Wor Barrow this familiar landmark was totally demolished, and the earth spoil from the excavation still lies in heaps where it was dumped outside the site. In his museum near Farnham village, Pitt-Rivers placed a model of the barrow showing the original positions of the objects found in it. He recorded everything meticulously and was an excellent surveyor, making the first contour plans of British earthworks and setting standards in archaeology which are respected to this day. But his records are no substitute for the earthworks themselves, and these, through his policy of entirely stripping a site, he levelled wholesale.

Opening of the tumulus at St Weonard's, Herefordshire, in 1855. Inside the mound, though not discovered on that occasion, are said to be the bones of the parish saint in a gold coffin. The site was a traditional meeting-place for dancing and festivals.

Meanwhile, and for decades to come, the same thing went on all over the country. Thomas Bateman in 1861 had written *Ten Years' Diggings in Celtic and Saxon Grave Hills*, an account of the vast number of barrows rifled by him and his father in Derbyshire, Staffordshire and Yorkshire. Canon William Greenwell, who published his *British Barrows* in 1877, went on opening barrows in Yorkshire and elsewhere until his death at the age of 98 in 1918. The activities of W.C. Borlase in the West Country have been mentioned earlier in the chapter on the Land's End.

The Pitt-Rivers technique of totally stripping sites under investigation was used by another military man, Colonel Hawley, in his excavations at Stonehenge during the 1920s, when, as Richard Atkinson writes in *Stonehenge*, 1965, the site was dug up like potatoes. Much of it was stripped to the bedrock, and its potential for yielding information to future investigators was destroyed for ever. Destruction by similar methods has been visited on the Glastonbury lake village, Silchester and many other interesting places.

The pity of it is that while important-looking sites have been subjected to detailed archaeological researches, many lesser antiquities have been lost without record; and the wastage continues up to the present day. Astronomer-archaeologists, to whom the shapes, positions and topographical relationships of ancient sites are more interesting than what is buried in them, have urged that archaeological efforts and resources be diverted from excavation to surveying. Everywhere there are still old stones and prehistoric relics which have yet to be recorded. These, no less than Stonehenge and other such famous sites, may have a crucial part to play in future inquiries into the megalithic enigma.

General Pitt-Rivers's mark: the medal he buried at every site he excavated.

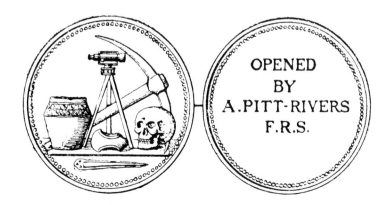

Above: Treasure hunting or early archaeological excavation at the Table des Marchands dolmen at Locmariaquer near Carnac, witnessed by Maudet de Penhouët at the beginning of the nineteenth century.

Caldwell County, North Carolina, 1882. The earth covering of a mound totally removed by archaeologist J.P. Rogan to reveal skeletons and stone vaulted graves. This figure was published in Cyrus Thomas's *Burial Mounds of the Northern Sections of the United States,* in which Thomas sought to demonstrate that the great mounds and earthworks across America were built by the ancestors of the indigenous Indians and not, as was commonly supposed, by a vanished race of giant stature. Rogan's mound did not, however, give him much support, because one of the skeletons, marked 16, was found to have been 'not less than 7 feet high when living'.

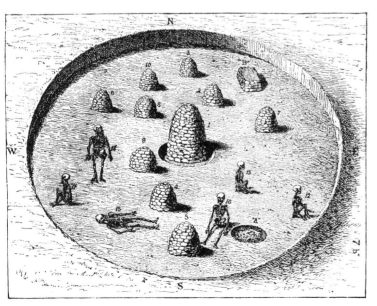

Above: A curious little book called *The Barrow Diggers* was written in 1839. Its anonymous author (identified by Mr L.V. Grinsell on the flyleaf of the copy he presented to the London Library as the Rev. C. Woolls, a Dorset antiquarian) had copies printed to give to friends who had assisted him at a recent excavation. It consists of a dialogue between barrow diggers in imitation of the gravedigger scene in *Hamlet,* and epitomizes the spirit of good-humoured dilettantism in which Colt Hoare and his neighbours set about their local antiquities. After a week's work the shaft was flooded by a spring. Nothing much was found but a glass bead and 'marks of cremation': just enough to show that it was not a *tumulus inanis* — barrow diggers' jargon for a mound with nothing in it.
North of Stonehenge, Colt Hoare and Cunnington were pictured (*right*) by Philip Crocker, directing operations at a barrow dig.

King Frederick VII of Denmark in the middle of the nineteenth century was a learned archaeologist and enthusiastic excavator. Here, comfortably seated with his pipe on a barrow in north Zealand, he supervises its demolition by soldiers.

Left: 'It was in the latter part of August of 1844,' wrote Thomas Wright in his *Wanderings of an Antiquary,* 'that I accompanied Lord Albert Conyngham (now Lord Londesborough) on a visit to the Friars at Aylesford, for the purpose of opening a large Roman barrow or supulchral mound in the adjoining parish of Snodland.' It was a country house party, consisting of local antiquaries, clergymen and ladies, and every morning their host had them rowed down the Medway to the site of the dig, where they passed the day feasting and playing while a dozen or so workmen cut up the mound. On one occasion there was a heavy shower, and the party protected itself in the ingenious manner which Wright here illustrates. To everyone's disappointment the mound yielded no treasure, but the rumour went around the neighbourhood that they had found gold, and a large party of locals was seen swarming over the mound as the excavators were leaving it.

Opposite and above: Photographs recording stages in General Pitt-Rivers's demolition of Wor Barrow, a former landmark in Cranborne Chase, Dorset. Wide trenches were first cut through the middle of the barrow, and finally the whole of the barrow was removed.

Below: Pitt-Rivers's 'Craniometer for measuring the profiles of skulls and living heads'. Before its recent fall from fashion, the practice of measuring ancient skulls and drawing conclusions about relative racial qualities therefrom played a considerable part in the archaeological process.

10 Stones with holes

The Tolvan stone of
Constantine, Corn-
wall, one of the last
places where the pre-
Christian rites of
infant baptism sur-
vived, as here illus-
trated by Joseph
Blight in about 1873.
Babies were passed
nine times through
the hole in the stone
and then laid to sleep
on a grassy knoll.
The Tolvan stone is
about nine feet tall,
and is thought to
have stood at the
entrance to a former
barrow or chamber,
like the example
opposite in France.

Here are illustrated some of these interesting monuments, the original purpose of which no one has yet succeeded in demonstrating. Many of them occur
in the vicinity of a stone circle, and Lockyer was convinced that they were part
of the apparatus of ancient observatories, used by Stone Age astronomers to
sight towards a definite point on the horizon. Unfortunately, the large number
of holed stones which have been destroyed or moved from their proper sites
has reduced the opportunities to test this theory. The famous Stone of Odin in
the Orkneys, perforated by a hole about five feet from the ground, which
Lockyer believed to have been used for seasonal observations of sunrise and
sunset, was removed in 1814 to put an end to the 'superstitious practices' pro-
voked by it. There is but one original sketch of it and no exact record of its position. In the case of the Men-an-tol stone in Cornwall Lockyer was equally
unlucky, because records show that at least one of the stones aligned with it to
indicate the May sunrise has been moved in modern times.

The outstanding feature of holed stones is that, in common with holy wells,
they have retained the old ideas and customs popularly associated with them
more tenaciously than any other kind of megalithic monument. These ideas
are universal. In India, as in northern Europe, the obvious symbolic connection between holed stones and childbirth is emphasized by the peasant custom
of passing babies through the hole. Various reasons are traditionally given for
this practice, as a cure or magical prevention of certain illnesses, but essentially it is an act of baptism or rebirth. 'The earliest peoples in Indian history
thought stones with holes in them were emblems of the *yoni*, and the ritual action of going through that hole implied a regeneration by means of the feminine cosmic principle,' writes Mircea Eliade in *Patterns of Comparative Religion*,
1958. But, he continues, 'these ring-stones in India have a certain solar symbolism in addition.' This is implied in the Indians' term for holed stones,

'gates of deliverance', meaning deliverance from the mundane cycle of rebirth rather than from the womb, and this achievement, says Eliade, 'is bound up with the symbolism of the sun'.

For a non-initiate, it is hard to evaluate statements such as these or to judge the extent to which ancient symbolism is relevant to modern enquiry into the original purpose of megalithic holed stones. Symbolism, however, relates to function, and the traditional association of holed stones with the sun appears thus to support the astronomical theories about these monuments. On the other hand, neither ancient lore nor any of the recorded customs at holed stones gives indications of their being used for astronomical observation. They were formerly attended by local people for a variety of purposes to do with fertility, therapy, betrothals, sealing bargains and so on, and although certain customs were related to the sun, they involved magical rather than astronomical performances. Thus at the Men-an-tol people seeking cures were supposed to pass through the ring three or nine times against the sun, and Orkney parents used to put their children through the hole in the Stone of Odin at Beltane and midsummer after having dipped them in a nearby holy well which they processed round sunwise. Lockyer believed that the popular use of holed stones for cures and pregnancies was a later development in times when their original astronomical use had lapsed, but there is no evidence for that in any of their legends, which are everywhere unanimous in calling them magical rather than astronomical devices. Holed stones, together with other types of megalithic structures, may have been orientated so as to allow the sun's rays to play a symbolic or effective part in seasonal ceremonies, rather than for observational purposes.

The Dolmen of Trie (Hautes-Pyrénées).

The restorative virtues of natural holes and clefts in stones, and the power of certain rocks to bring about pregnancies, were common beliefs long before the age of megalith building. Evidently, the artificially holed stones at ancient ritual centres had the same virtues as those naturally holed. That must surely have been the reason why they were set up in the first place. In Eliade's summary of the Eastern traditions relating to holed stones, they are associated first with the yin or feminine cosmic principle, corresponding with the vital energies of the earth, and secondly with the power of the sun. That implies, first, that these stones were sited, as sacred monuments were traditionally sited, by augurs and geomancers, in conjunction with centres of the earth's magnetic current, and, secondly, that they were designed to receive the rays of the sun at certain times of the year. The intended effects of the rituals centred upon them were probably very similar to those specified in the surviving traditions about holed stones, which in general identify them as instruments for promoting fertility. A further use by the priesthood in connection with their doctrines of rebirth and liberation of the soul is also suggested.

The Church and the age of reason have destroyed almost every remnant of the faith which derived babies and good health from certain rocks with holes through them. The nineteenth-century scholars who recorded the last of the old customs were unanimous in describing them as ignorant superstitions. No one even thought of inquiring whether these absurd rustic performances actually worked. As the scientific study of megalithic monuments intensifies, that is one of the questions which will doubtless attract the attention of future researchers.

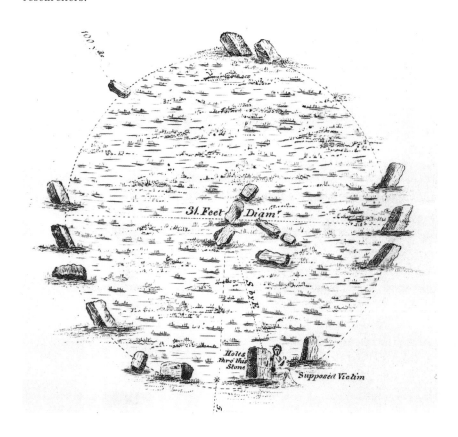

Opposite: Holed stones are often found near stone circles, and Dr Borlase believed that they might have been used for securing the Druids' victims before the moment of sacrifice. The idea was illustrated in 1820 by Robert Knox in his view of a 'Druid-temple on Cloughton Moor' in east Yorkshire.

Above: A rare, but by contemporary accounts not a very accurate record of the holed Stone of Odin in Orkney, made by Elizabeth Leveson-Gower in 1807. About seven years later it was removed by the local farmer, angered by tourists.

Below left: The Clach-a-Charra stone at Onich, Lochaber, Inverness-shire.

Below right: The Trevethy Quoit, once known as the Giant's House, in St Cleer, east Cornwall, has a hole drilled through its capstone, for which no one has yet suggested any good reason.

Three examples, in late nineteenth century illustrations from Carthailac, of dolmens in Portugal, the Crimea and the Caucasus, with small holes carefully cut to their interiors. The purpose or purposes of these holes is a matter of speculation. Among the suggestions are: passages for the spirits of the dead, windows for communication with anchorites, devices connected with oracles or initiation, and spy-holes for astronomical observation. In the case of the Caucasian dolmen, the low rounded hole at ground level supports the belief implied in its name: the House of Dwarfs.

Above: The Speckled or Grey Stone at Tobernavean near Sligo. It stands at the junction of three parishes by a tiny stream. Diseased children were once pushed through its hole as a cure.

Right: The Long Stone at Minchinhampton, Gloucestershire, perforated with several natural holes. One of these was said to have the usual property of healing sick children put through it. Other legends about it, as summarized by L.V. Grinsell, include its defying all attempts to move it and the tendency of a phantom black dog to appear in its vicinity.

The Long Stone.
Minchinhampton

Edl. Burrow. 1913

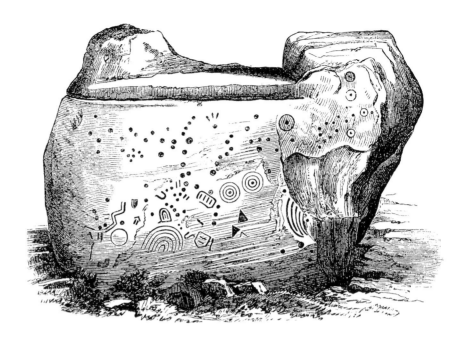

11 Ancient rock carvings, and some freaks of interpretation

An illustration from E.A. Conwell's *The Tomb of Ollamh Fodhla*, 1874. Outside the supposed tomb of this ancient Irish king, which Conwell discovered in County Meath, is an inscribed rock curiously shaped in the form of a seat, which is popularly called the Hag's Chair. Conwell recognized it as the judgment seat of the old king and renamed it Ollamh Fodhla's Chair. The symbols inscribed on it, clearly shown here, have now almost entirely vanished.

As many poets have exclaimed, there is a striking contrast between the solid physical presence of megalithic monuments and their total silence about their own meaning. Yet it may be that they are not so uncommunicative as at first sight appears, for the rocks at many prehistoric sites are inscribed with carved symbols, and if only one could discover the codes behind them a great deal of detailed information would immediately become available. Many attempts have been made at interpreting prehistoric rock inscriptions, and the modern resurgence of megalithomania has added significantly to their number. Several books on the subject have recently been published. New clues have been discovered, and the ancient carvings are now being investigated more intensively than ever before.

Many natural rock formations and megalithic stones in northern England, Scotland and Ireland are inscribed with cup-and-ring and other symbols, of which some typical examples are here illustrated. The simplest of these markings is the cup or shallow pit, sometimes surrounded by one or more circles or forming the centre of a spiral figure. In many cases a line has been carved from outside the design to the central cup, suggesting the labyrinth symbol, and the labyrinth is made explicit in several examples, as at Tintagel. With these images are associated other characteristic markings, such as lozenges, sunray patterns and serpentine lines. Similar designs occur in other European countries, in America, and on sacred rocks and objects of the Aborigines in Australia. It would seem therefore that they have some universal meaning in relation to the lives and mental patterns of nomadic people.

The most intriguing of prehistoric rock inscriptions are those found within the stone-lined chambers and passages of western Europe, particularly those of Ireland. The most wonderful collection is displayed about thirty miles north of Dublin at the great chambered mounds (unjustifiably referred to by archaeologists as 'tombs' in a stone-age 'necropolis') on the bank of the river Boyne. The three largest mounds, New Grange, Knowth and Dowth, are surrounded at their bases by rings of curb stones, flat slabs carefully set up on edge, and many of these, particularly at Knowth, are ornamented with a magnificent range of carved symbols or patterns, which occur also on the stone slabs of the mounds' inner chambers and passages. As the finest of all collections of megalithic sculpture they are rivalled only by the examples at Gavrinnis in Brittany and by the more stylized carvings in the prehistoric temples of Malta. New Grange and the Maltese structures are now reckoned to be roughly contemporary, 5,000 or more years old, while the French claim even greater antiquity for some of their monuments.

It is not much more than a hundred years ago since people began to notice and speculate about the ancient British rock carvings, but antiquarians have more than made up for the late start by the amazing variety of theories they have subsequently advanced in explanation of them. The first to draw public attention to them, the Rev. William Greenwell, in an unpublished lecture to the Architectural Institute at Newcastle in 1852, was inclined to see them as sacred symbols designed to 'record some divine truth'. He also thought that they might be records of local burials. A popular early theory was that they were maps of ancient camps and settlements, whose plans are indeed similar to the concentric circle carvings. This idea occured to Bishop Graves, who noticed the rock carvings in Ireland almost simultaneously with Greenwell in Northumberland. Maps of the heavens were another suggestion, with pits surrounded by circles representing the sun, crescent shapes or plain circles the moon, wavy lines the Milky Way and so on. G.V. Du Noyer, who with E.A. Conwell first recorded the inscribed stones of chambered mounds in the Loughcrew mountains of Ireland, wrote to the *Meath Herald* (21 October 1865) that 'one of the groups of small hollows very closely resembles the constellation of the Plough'. The star chart interpretation was most fully developed in 1921 by Bishop Browne who found that certain cup-marked rocks in Aberdeenshire formed maps of the constellations in mirror image, suggesting that the ancient astronomers took rubbings or impressions of them. Some authorities have seen the ancient carvings as types of early writing, while others have contrived to fit them into pet theories as relating to Druid sacrifices, sex rites, metal prospectors' signs, masons' marks and much else besides. No less than twenty-five different published explanations of cup-and-ring markings have recently been summarized by Ronald Morris, in the *Transactions of the Ancient Monuments Society*, vol. 16, to delight connoisseurs of archaeological theories. Some of them seem plausible enough, but there is no single theory which can reasonably be applied to the whole range of prehistoric rock carvings.

The tendency of archaeologists throughout the first half of this century to discourage theories and speculations and to accept only the evidence turned up by their spades – a fashion which almost killed archaeology as a subject of popular interest – inhibited further studies of the carvings on ancient sites and monuments. It became conventional to regard them as meaningless ornament or as early essays in 'art', and to compare them to the scribblings of children or to the contrived primitivism of modern painters like Picasso. Archaeologists set themselves up as art critics, often with unfortunate results. Thus Michael Herity in his classic work, *Irish Passage Graves*, 1974, finds fault with the ancient sculptor of one of the chambered cairns at Loughcrew on the grounds that he failed to achieve 'true harmony', while allowing that he had at least carried out his basic intention, 'the depiction of a number of standard magical

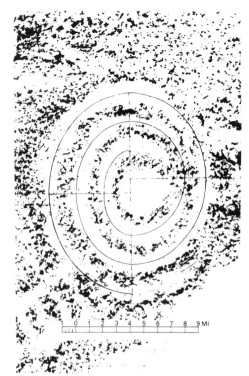

Above left: From a rubbing by Evan Hadingham of a spiral carved on the Panorama Stone at Ilkley, Yorkshire, Alexander Thom obtained this version of the sculptor's original design. The scale is in megalithic inches, and the spiral is set out in integers of that unit.

Above right: The first photograph, taken at noon on midsummer day, 1978, of the dagger of sunlight which, at that unique moment, cuts through the centre of a spiral carved on a rock face at Fajada Butte, New Mexico.

motifs in a pleasant arrangement'. Others saw in the ancient carvings the first attempts at representational art and claimed to recognize in their patterns the features of goddesses, battle scenes and so on.

The first serious contribution to their study in this generation was made by Professor Thom in 1968. In an article in the Gurdjieffian magazine, *Systematics*, he showed that the circular and spiral patterns on rocks in northern Britain were carefully set out with fixed compasses in units of measure which he called the megalithic inch, its value (0.068 foot) being equal to a fortieth part of the megalithic yard (2.72 feet), or a hundredth part of the megalithic rod (6.8 feet). These designs he found to be small-scale models of stone circle groundplans, drawn from the same canon of Pythagorean geometry as were the works of megalithic architecture. Where they occur on rocks featuring in astronomical alignments, Thom suggested that they encode information about the use of megalithic observatories.

Similar astronomical clues to the meaning of ancient rock markings have recently been found in many parts of North America. The most spectacular discovery was made by an artist, Anna Sofaer, in Chaco Canyon, New Mexico. She was with a party engaged in recording rock carvings in the Canyon, which was inhabited up to about AD 1200 by people of a mysterious civilization, called by the modern Pueblo Indians the Anasazi, 'the ancient folk'. The stone structures, including large apartment blocks, of these people, their system of long, perfectly straight roads, and the evidence of astronomical orientations in their buildings and monuments are now attracting much attention from American students of native astronomy. Claims have been made that several of the local groups of rock carvings were designed as records or indicators of astronomical events.

Just before noon on 29 June 1977, Anna Sofaer had made the perilous ascent of a high, sandstone formation, the Fajada Butte, on the top of which are several carvings, including a group of two spirals picked out on a rock face and sheltered by three great stone slabs. As she looked at the larger of the two spirals, the sun reached its highest point in the heavens, and a thin dagger of light penetrated through the crack between two of the slabs and struck through the spiral, just to the right of its centre. It was a few days after the summer solstice, and the following year, at noon on the longest day, a party of scientists were on the butte to observe and photograph the ray of light as it passed vertically along the axis and exactly through the centre of the spiral. Further research proved that not only the summer solstice but the other quarter days were marked by unique patterns of light rays in relation to the carvings. The function of the spiral images as a sundial indicator of noon at different seasons thus seems to have been established, providing the first clear interpretation of an ancient rock carving anywhere in the world.

The most significant advance in decoding the symbols of ancient rock carvings has recently been made in Ireland. It has been known for some years that at dawn on the shortest day of the year a ray of sunlight penetrates the inner chamber at New Grange, shining straight down the narrow passage through a rectangular, stone-framed slit above the entrance. In *The Boyne Valley Vision*, 1980, Martin Brennan claimed that the two chambers at Knowth, one facing east, the other west, were illuminated by sunrise and sunset at the equinoxes. This was confirmed by observation in 1980 at the autumn equinox, and Brennan went on to show that the inner chamber at Dowth received light at midwinter sunset.

Similar orientations towards the sun and moon of chambers and passages in mounds all over Ireland have been identified by Brennan and his colleague, Jack Roberts, whose observations disclosed a feature, previously unnoticed, of the carvings on the mounds' inner and curb stones. Many of these are illuminated or picked out by a shadow from sun or moonlight at certain days of the year, and this has provided the clue from which Brennan has begun his interpretation of the ancient carved symbols. On the summit of the Loughcrew hills in County Meath the mound called by Conwell 'The Tomb of Ollamh Fodhla', now prosaically known as Cairn T, has its interior passage orientated

Two inscribed stones from the Tomb of Ollamh Fodhla, as figured by Conwell.

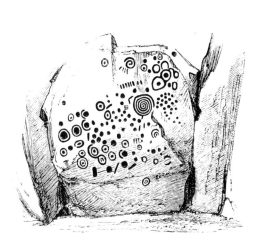
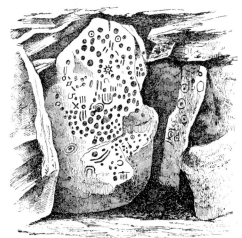

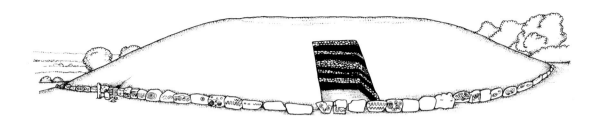

Martin Brennan's
drawing, made in
1980, of the hill of
Knowth, with a
section cut away to
show details of its
construction. Many
of the stone slabs in
the ring round the
base of the mound
are inscribed with
mysterious designs.

towards the equinoctial sunrise. A watcher inside the chamber at dawn sees
the entry of a thin, bright sunray which strikes the ornamented stones on the
back wall and moves steadily across their faces, picking out one by one the
various inscribed symbols. The effect is of a moving finger of light, spelling out
a story in an unknown language, relating perhaps to astronomical or astrolog-
ical lore, to cosmogony, to the myths and histories of the race, or to a combina-
tion of these and other themes. To aid the interpreter the sun itself is identifying its own symbols.

Significant shadow effects have also been observed in connection with megalithic carvings. At Knowth, for example, as the time of the equinox approaches, the shadow of an upright stone at sunset falls onto an inscribed
stone at the western entrance. A vertical line carved down the centre of this
stone marks the centre line of the passage, and on the day when the sun sets at
the mid-point of its yearly course, the edge of the shadow cast by the standing
stone falls precisely onto the carved line.

In recording the seasonal interplay between light and shadow and the symbols on ornamented stones Brennan claims to have found astronomical references in certain of the symbols, relating them to aspects of the heavenly
bodies. Their further interpretation, however, presents enormous difficulties,
particularly under present conditions. For the Irish monuments are now in a
far worse state than they were even a hundred years ago when they were generally respected by local people on account of their reputation as the haunts of
spirits who would visit ill fortune on anyone violating their sites. That spell
was broken, often together with the monuments themselves, by the archaeological excavators, whose investigations have frequently destroyed the subtle
stone arrangements which permitted narrow light beams to penetrate a subterranean mound-chamber and emphasize a succession of its carved symbols.
Only a few years ago New Grange was scientifically dug into, many of its interior and other stones were disturbed, and the reconstructed model, now curiously faced with a layer of ornamental pebble-dash of quartz and boulders to
represent someone's theory of how it originally looked, lets in rain through the
roof for the first time in history. Other important monuments are similarly
threatened with excavation. A conflict of interests thus arises between excavators of megalithic monuments and those who seek to interpret them by other
means. Yet, for all such complaints, there remains a vast amount of material
to challenge the wits of as many researchers as care to take up the most fascinating aspect of megalithic studies, the deciphering of ancient rock carvings.

No book dealing with megalithomania would be complete without a reference
to a few of the hilarious incidents which have been occasioned by scholars
specializing in the translation of ancient inscriptions. The most famous of these
was Professor the Abbé Breuil, who excelled in the art of discerning faces, fig-

ures and whole series of ancient rock images where others could see only abstract patterns or natural cracks and crevices. Breuil identified chthonic deities and spirit guardians in the spiral designs of chambered cairns and recognized the features of goddesses in cup-and-ring marks, particularly where there were carved wavy lines which might be taken to represent hair. He acquired a distinguished following among archaeologists. Many of the writings on prehistoric rock carvings, published during the present century, are enlivened by the authors' interpretations of the primitive representational or stylized images which they have detected in these 'early art works'.

A good example, to which attention is drawn in Evan Hadingham's *Ancient Carvings in Britain*, 1974, is Professor R.A.S. Macalister's reading of a boulder at Clonfinlough. Its face, as shown here from his *Ireland in Pre-Celtic Times*, 1921, is covered with enigmatic markings, including figures like the Greek Φ. Macalister explained these as members of a tribe, engaged in battle with other warriors who are represented by the crosses. Among the latter are marks resembling footprints, which indicate that they are running away, and the cup marks around them are the severed heads which they have lost to the enemy! Hadingham comments that, apart from the oval shapes, most of the markings on the Clonfinlough boulder appear to be natural effects of rainwater.

The very heights of inspired lunacy have been achieved by experts in dead languages confronted with ancient rock markings. One of the most lauded feats of translation in the nineteenth century was that of the Icelandic runic expert, Professor Finn Magnusson, at the Runamo rock in Sweden, which had been famous among scholars since the Middle Ages for the extensive inscriptions etched upon it in an unknown ancient script. In 1833 Magnusson led an expedition set up by the Danish Royal Society, which spent the summer encamped

The 'carved' rock at Clonfinlough, County Offaly.

Professor Magnusson's expedition of 1833 working at the site of the Runamo runes in Sweden. From his reading of the markings on a strip of rock, Magnusson produced a distinguished work of literature in the form of five heroic poems from prehistoric times. The poems delighted Scandinavian scholars, but the markings from which they were taken were later proved by geologists to consist of natural fissures in the rock surface.

The 'runes' on the Runamo Rock: an engraving of 1841 after a survey by Danish scholars.

near the rock for the purpose of making accurate copies of the inscribed characters. This accomplished, Magnusson set about translating them, and the following year his finished version was published in the Royal Society's *Proceedings*. It caused an immediate sensation throughout Scandinavia, for the inscription, read from right to left, had proved to consist of five poems in an ancient metre known as *fornyrdislag*, composed to celebrate the victory of Harald Hildetand over King Sigurd Ring. Magnusson had thus identified the only original document relating to the legendary battle of Bråvalla, and from the style of the verses he was even able to suggest the identity of the poet, a royal bard named Starkoddr.

A few years later, however, Magnusson's triumph was spoilt by Swedish geologists who made a different interpretation of the Runamo inscription as being made up of natural lines and cracks in the rock surface. This subsequently proved to be the case, and poor Magnusson was mocked. It was suggested that since the 'inscription' was supposed to be in a secret language of which he claimed to be the only interpreter, and since many of the markings were so faint that their significance was a matter of selection, there was plenty of opportunity for self-delusion and he had fallen victim to his own theories. Yet up to the time of his death Magnusson continued to insist that his version was the correct one, and he called in evidence the unanimous judgment of literary scholars that he had added a true masterpiece to early Scandinavian literature. No one has ever disputed its fine quality.

The celebrated Grave Creek stone, dug out of a mound near the Ohio river in 1838, has given employment to generations of antiquarian linguists. According to the Tenth Annual Report of the Smithsonian Bureau of Ethnology, Washington, 1893, the marks on this stone have been so variously interpreted that 'one scholar finds among them four characters which he claims are ancient Greek; another claims that four are Etruscan; five have been said to be Runic; six, ancient Gaelic; seven, old Erse; ten, Phoenician; fourteen, old British; and sixteen, Celtiberic. M. Lévy Bing reported to the Congress of Americanists at Nancy, in 1875, that he found in the inscription twenty-three Canaanite letters.'

The same high standards of imaginative scholarship as were displayed in the debate over the language of the Grave Creek stone have been maintained in its translation. M. Lévy Bing told the Americanists that its meaning in Canaanite was:

'What thou sayest, thou dost impose it, thou shinest in thy impetuous élan and rapid chamois.'

In 1857 M. Maurice Schwab had published an alternative rendering of the inscription:

'The Chief of Emigration who reached these places (or this island) has fixed these statutes forever.'

Other interpretations have been offered by M. Oppert and, recently, by Professor Barry Fell of Harvard University. They are:

'The grave of one who was assassinated here. May God to avenge him strike his murderer, cutting off the hand of his existence.' (Oppert)

'The mound raised-on-high for Tasach

'This tile

'[His] queen caused-to-be-made.' (Fell)

Professor Fell identifies the language of the Grave Creek stone as Spanish Punic of the first millennium BC. On the back of his 1976 book, *America BC*, Fell is described as 'one of the greatest decipherers of all time'. Much of his work is

Excavated from the Ohio mound (illustrated on page 49) in 1838, the Grave Creek tablet has baffled a host of learned interpreters; and no wonder, since the images of it, published for scholarly analysis, have been so remarkably at variance with each other and with the original. The first example, above, was referred to by M. Jomard of Paris when he declared that the characters were derived from the Phoenician language; the one below was sent in the same year, 1843, to Professor Rafn in Copenhagen, who merely stated that the letters were definitely not Runic.

published in the journals of his Epigraphy Society, and in these can be found inscriptions from ancient relics and rocks translated from many languages with the absolute certainty that distinguished the earlier works of Bing, Schwab, Oppert et al. And he is a worthy successor to the Abbé Breuil in perceiving ancient artefacts in objects marked or shaped by nature, some of which are illustrated in his book. It should be added, however, that American scholars have long been inclined to dismiss as forgeries all objects and inscriptions that indicate pre-colonial contact between America and Europe or the East, often on no better grounds than their own prejudices. Some of these relics, excavated by Fell from museum basements, do indeed seem to support his thesis that such contacts were more widespread than has generally been supposed.

Finally, to illustrate the most basic difficulty that scholars have had to face in interpreting ancient inscriptions, here is a collection of representations of one and the same original, which is an erratic boulder lying in the Taunton river, Massachusetts, known as the Dighton Writing Rock on account of the characters carved on its surface. All these versions have been published at different times in learned societies' journals or sent for translation to distinguished scholars in Europe. Many of these positively identified the script as Scythian, Phoenician, Oriental, Runic and so on, and a Scandinavian antiquary read it as a memorial to Thorfinn the Hopeful. Local experts recognize the characters as Algonquin. There seems to be enough evidence here to support anyone's theory.

Some of the amazingly different transcriptions of the Dighton Writing Rock in Massachusetts which have given scholars a wide latitude in translating its characters.

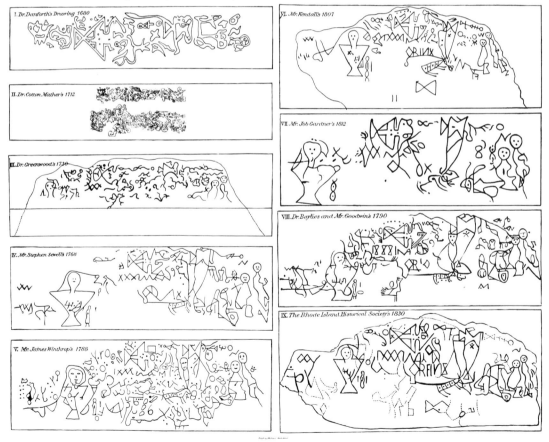

Left: Early records of 1867, from drawings by Mossman, of one of the inscriptions at Routing Lynn, Northumberland, and, *below* , an inscribed rock surface at Old Bewick, Northumberland.

Above: The group of moorland rocks, inscribed with ancient markings, at Routing Lynn, Northumberland. From a drawing of 1867.

New Grange, in County Meath, before excavation (*left*), in its
former character as the fairy hill and the haunt of Irish
mythologists, poets and picnickers. The identity of the figures,
photographed at the beginning of this century at the entrance to
its chamber, is unknown.

Above: Christopher Castle's drawing of the New Grange front
kerbstone, the entrance to its passage and, above it, the stone-
framed 'light-box' which admits a ray of sunlight into the inner
chamber at midwinter.

Below: New Grange transformed in recent years into an
archaeological show-site after undergoing drastic excavations.

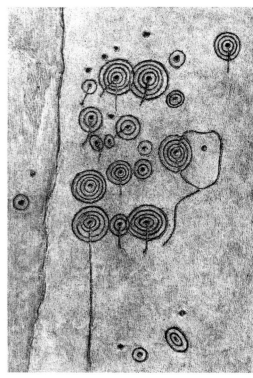

Some of the early records of cup marks, concentric rings and other motifs of prehistoric design on monuments and rock faces in the north of England, reproduced in J.Y. Simpson's *Archaic Sculpturings*, 1867.

Opposite, above: Stones of the former passage and chamber of the ruined mound at Knockmany, County Tyrone, inscribed with symbols which may have been designed for 'reading' in connection with seasonal patterns of sunlight. Here, as at so many of the important Irish sites, details of the original construction of the monument and other vital evidence towards the interpretation of these markings have been lost for ever.

Opposite, below: The classical labyrinth found in north Cornwall, near the coast at Rocky Valley, Tintagel. There is no certain way of dating such a carving; the consensus of specialists' opinions makes it prehistoric.

Yet to be deciphered are the extraordinary groups of earthen effigies, representing various animals, mythological creatures and human figures, which extend across wide areas of Wisconsin and the upper Mississippi valley, often situated on high plateaux. These examples are near McGregor, Iowa. The effigies are raised only a few feet above the level of the ground, making it impossible to see the whole of any group other than from the air — and then only when the low sun casts a shadow. For these photographs, taken in the 1970s, the effigies were outlined in lime.

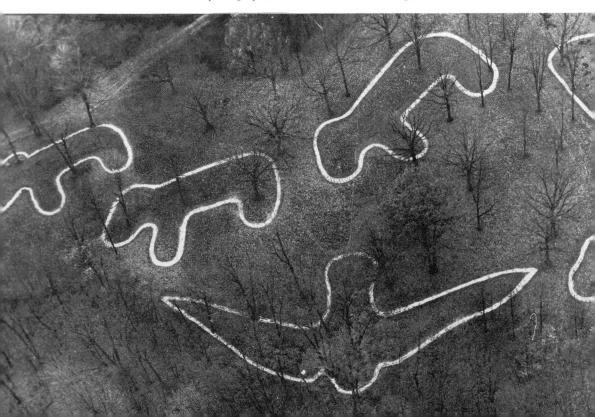

12   Survivals and revivals:
the modern significance of megalithic sites

One of the reasons for modern interest in the works and activities of the megalith builders of Europe is that they have had a fundamental influence on the forms of modern life and culture. The lore, legends and local customs of the countryside, the dates and places of festivals, fairs and seasonal gatherings and other traditional components in pre-industrial culture were to a great extent inherited from prehistoric times, and the enduring parts of this inheritance are the sites and landmarks which have retained a sacred or legendary significance over several thousand years up to the present. Parish churches for example are, probably in most cases, built on sites of pre-Christian sanctuaries, often on or within megalithic mounds, earthworks or stone circles. Thus the siting of churches and of the villages that grew up around them has been largely determined by the megalith builders, whose monuments and trackways have also contributed to the pattern of roads, boundaries and settlements of the modern landscape.

In all historical accounts of Christianity or any new religion supplanting another, the practice of the new church has always been to take over and reconsecrate the temples and sanctuaries of the former establishment. This is certainly an old custom, for it is specifically recommended by Plato in the *Republic,* and examples of its more recent observance include the systematic erection of Christian churches and crosses on the sites of native shrines throughout Latin America.

153

The proportion of old churches in Britain built on pagan sites is difficult to estimate. At many church sites no evidence is visible, and there are obvious inhibitions to excavation. Among the indications of christianized prehistoric sites, as given in Walter Johnson's *Byways in British Archaeology*, 1912, are the following: churches on mounds, or in raised, circular churchyards, or within ancient earthworks; menhirs, mounds or holy wells in the vicinity of churches; large boulders, foreign to the district, in a church's foundations or altar; and churches on high places, often dedicated to St Michael. Additional to these is the folklore record, in which legends of churches moved to their present positions by supernatural forces, or sited through visions or divination, suggest that the spots eventually chosen were already sanctified by the previous religion. In Ireland, it is said, over half the old churches share their sites with prehistoric stones or holy wells; and the great number of English churches which appear to rest on pre-Christian foundations allows that Alfred Watkins may have been right in supposing that almost all churches before the Reformation were so placed. This, he claimed, was the reason why so many churches stand in direct line with each other, having replaced the earlier monuments which marked the course of leys or prehistoric trackways.

Investigation of Watkins's ley theory has renewed interest in Christianity's inheritance of the old sacred places and megalithic sites. In many cases he observed that not only churches but old manor houses, stone crosses, wells, ponds, fords, groves, crossroads and other such minor landmarks in the old-fashioned countryside stood in alignments with each other, thus indicating prehistoric origins which were often confirmed by inspection. It is an idea to stimulate the imagination that the mysterious pattern of stone monuments and earthworks, imposed on the landscape of prehistoric Britain, has been essentially preserved through the continued use of the old sites for religious or other purposes. It is not so much the architectural qualities of old churches and villages but the subtly appropriate ways in which they relate to their natural surroundings that have produced the harmonious effect so often remarked upon in the rural landscape; and this effect must to some extent be attributed to the work of the prehistoric surveyors or geomancers by whom so many of the sites of local shrines, settlements and traditional places of assembly were first selected. To them also must be attributed the origins of the native European cultures, which developed in landscapes whose shape and character had been formed by the megalith builders.

It is natural therefore that people who engage themselves in promoting cultural revivals or reinvigorating local traditions should look back into prehistoric times for the ideals they wish to see re-established. The classic example is William Stukeley, whose antiquarian researches became inextricably mixed with his plans for a world-wide revival of true religion, resulting in his peopling megalithic sites with sage Druid priests, designed to reflect his ideal picture of theocratic authority. Stukeley's influence, transmitted through his prophet, William Blake, remains powerful; but independent of it, existing on a popular level, is a native tradition of the Druids and their sacred places as symbols of resistance to tyranny. Many of the manorial moots and open-air courts in Saxon times were still held at megalithic sites, which are thus associated in the minds of revivalists with the native rights and liberties extinguished with the imposition of the 'Norman yoke'. As recently as 1839 the disaffected Chartists, whose principal demand was the restoration of the old Anglo-Saxon constitution, held occasional meetings at the mounds and hilltop enclosures which ancient custom had appointed as places of festival and

Oldbury Camp
or Outpost. with
Oldbury Church

The village church at Oldbury, overlooking the Severn estuary in Gloucestershire, stands on an ancient mound surrounded by the earthworks of Oldbury Camp. The artist, E.J. Burrow (another of his drawings is shown on page 137), was active in the early part of this century, and published some delightful series of drawings to illustrate the great earthworks of Gloucestershire and Somerset.

public gathering. Almost all such festivals and many of their sites were destroyed by enclosures of common lands and by the various other such processes which have wasted away the independence and culture of whole regions throughout Britain and beyond.

This has not simply been a function of economics. A considerable factor in regional decline has been the tendency of learned men of the dominant culture to discourage the cultural pretensions of the minor districts and nations. The cause of this may be political, or it may arise from assumptions of national or racial superiority. Thus Dr Johnson denounced the poems of Ossian as obvious modern fabrications because such heroic themes could not possibly have been produced or memorized by the barbaric Scots. Similarly treated by the English scholars were the ancient Welsh bardic records, written down or transcribed by Iolo Morgannwg, the last of the initiated Glamorgan bards, at the end of the eighteenth century; and the professors of the Welsh universities have commonly acquiesced in the denigration of their own native traditions.

In regions where the significant landmarks of local topography are eradicated or forgotten, together with their accumulated patina of lore, traditions and common observances, the country becomes dull and spiritless and can no longer be decently inhabited, and rural depopulation duly follows. As a substitute for locally rooted culture the centrally directed variety now offered is inadequate, not only because it necessarily tends towards the lowest common denominator, but because it gives no guarantee of continuity. The meaning, as here used, of the word culture is the art of being reconciled to one's surroundings, both natural and man-made. In that sense the purest form of culture is that of nomadic peoples, whose only possession it is and who live by their cultures entirely. The traditional sacred places of all countries were first marked off in times before settlement as places of seasonal tribal gatherings, and thus they are reminders of the ancient cultures in which our own are still rooted.

Every culture is umbilically linked with its native countryside. The maintenance of those links is necessary for its survival, and, as Stukeley perceived, it can only be renewed by strengthening them. For that purpose Stukeley created a myth, so well founded that it has endured to this day, by which Stonehenge became a temple of the ancestral Druids and a prime symbol of national culture. His myth succeeded because it was in accordance with tradition on two levels, popular and poetic. Generations of academics since Stukeley have tried to stamp out the popular notion which associates megalithic monuments with Druids, but in vain; and on the literary level Stukeley's picture of a magical civilization in far antiquity is in the same line of esoteric tradition which, as Kathleen Raine points out in her work on Blake, has always inspired poets, despite the disapproval of their academic commentators.

From the time of its conception Stukeley's myth has always had a rival which, in contrast to his, reflects belief in evolutionary progress and a primitive view of antiquity as concisely expresssed by Hobbes (quoted on page 101). According to the rival myth megalithic monuments were merely places of burial or superstitious rites by unknown savages. Archaeologists from the second half of the nineteenth century, with their professional faith in excavation as the only legitimate method of interpreting prehistoric sites, have presented a solid front in maintaining that myth. But its disadvantages and inadequacies have now become obvious. In the first place, it fails to reflect the results of modern megalithic research by astronomers and others, and the picture of ancient society derived from them. Secondly, it has tended to inhibit creative approaches to the megalithic mystery by ruling out the possibility that there could be anything of contemporary scientific interest to be learnt from the works of our primitive ancestors. Finally, it has had the effect of dehumanizing and secularizing the ancient places of the countryside, of detaching them from the traditions and local lore that had accumulated around them, and depriving them of all but academic significance.

In the interests of both truth and expediency a new myth is required. The wide range of its possible components is indicated by the variety of theories which people have draped round prehistoric monuments, as exemplified in earlier chapters of this book; and the recent spate of megalithic studies has added considerably to their number. The modern tendency has been to invest Stukeley's ancient sages with further qualities by representing them as skilful astronomers, geomancers, dowsers etc., and to attribute to the sites of their monuments certain geological or magnetic properties which marked them out as natural centres of magical operations. This approach to megalithic sites acknowledges the long continuity of human experience in which they feature as haunts of fairies, ghosts and phantom creatures. Many examples of such reports from earlier times are included in L.V. Grinsell's *Folklore of Prehistoric Sites in Britain*, 1976, but Grinsell takes the old conventional attitude to such things, that they are relics of the superstitions of a simpler age, unrelated to modern experience. He therefore omits any mention of similar types of phenomena reported in the present day. For this he was taken to task by the folklorist, S.F. Bigger *(Wiltshire Folklife* journal, Spring 1978), who quoted recent press items on UFO sightings around Stonehenge as examples of the weird events, experiences or notions which occur spontaneously in association with megalithic monuments and are therefore part of their legitimate tradition. This accords with the new approach of writers such as Janet and Colin Bord, whose book, *The Secret Country*, 1976, combines the traditional with modern evidence to show how persistent is the reputation of ancient sites as locations of strange forces and phenomena. Further research on these lines is suggested in Devereux and Thomson's *Ley Hunter's Companion*, 1979, and a recent book by Anthony Roberts, *Sowers of Thunder,* 1978, develops the same idea of probing the mysteries of the ancient science through an inclusive method of studying landscapes, which he calls 'geomythics'. This involves correlating the distribution of ancient sites with the incidence of geological faults, underground streams and veins of metals, with maps of local magnetic variations, with meteorological anomalies and spots attractive to lightning, and with ancient and modern folklore records.

With its recognition of the subtle forces in nature which condition people's experience of their localities, geomythics derives from a similar attitude to landscape to that which underlies systems of native mysticism all over the world. In Japanese Shintoism, for example, spots distinguished by lightning strikes or any other kind of portentous event are marked off as sacred or forbidden reservations, and Shinto sanctuaries are founded in relation to such places. The Roman augurs had similar practices, and there is evidence enough to make it a reasonable hypothesis that the European megalith builders sited their monuments in accordance with a comparable code of divination, designed to reveal the hidden aspects of nature as affecting human life. In that case, the many-sided geomythical approach to the mystery of prehistoric sites is appropriate.

But Roberts's antiquarianism, like Stukeley's, is directed towards objects which are far from merely academic. In the reappraisal of native traditions in the light of modern discoveries about the quality of prehistoric culture he sees the key to a national renaissance of millennial proportions. In the manner of Blake he invokes the spirit of Albion, guardian of the British landscape, to the end that 'the people of these islands can once more regain the pride of their true historical continuity and identity' and achieve 'an equal community of souls in harmony with the land and its magic'. Thus is continued the prophecy of William Stukeley, immortalized by Blake, that in Britain would be made the first reformation leading to the resanctification of the whole earth – a prophecy which transcends national chauvinism in allowing that all peoples should claim special destinies within the grand scheme through reconciliation with their native traditions and culture. In this spirit Blake's poem in *Jerusalem*, inserted into his address to the Jews, ends with the verse:

> *In my Exchanges every Land*
> *Shall walk, & mine in every Land,*
> *Mutual shall build Jerusalem:*
> *Both heart in heart & hand in hand.*

As a conventional explanation for megalithic monuments, the traditional, idealizing account, beloved alike by poets and common people, is more delightful and no less in accordance with established facts than any other. And it may, at the present time, be the most expedient. Through their folklore and legends the works of the megalith builders are everywhere associated with ancient knowledge of the earth and its spirit. From those legends, supported by modern research, there is now emerging a new myth of the stone age as a time when the interests of the living earth were closely studied and held sacred. That this myth largely reflects modern ecological concerns is undoubted, but it is none the less tenable for that; and all who share those concerns may welcome the new theory of antiquity which provides so useful a model for harmonious relations between this earth and the science of the future.

S. del. Aquatinted

Grand Conventional  *Festival of the Britons.*

Left: The 'Grand Conventional Festival of the Britons' at Stonehenge, splendidly imagined by Charles Hamilton Smith in 1815. The source of his inspiration is acknowledged in the small image at the foot of the picture showing Stukeley's serpent temple.

Below: Almost contemporary with Smith's view of an imaginary Stonehenge festival is Joseph Peacock's painting of an actual festival at an ancient sacred site, the Festival of the Seven Churches at Glendalough, depicted in about 1813.

The benefits which, until recently, country people derived from seasonal visits to certain rocks and megalithic sites were also associated with other local landmarks, such as wells, crossroads and notable trees. Among the relics of a lingering native tradition, illustrated in the middle of the nineteenth century, are a crossroads shrine attended by Breton peasants, and the chapel in the sacred oak at Allouville, Normandy.

Above: Dr G.W. MacGregor Reid, the 'Anointed Chosen Chief', sternly defended the tradition of a Druid ceremony at the stones on midsummer morning. At dawn on 21 June 1914, according to the *Salisbury Journal* of 27 June, 'Superintendent Buchanan of the Wiltshire Constabulary called his attention to the notice posted within Stonehenge prohibiting the holding of any form of meeting or service within the circle, and requested him to desist.... Dr Reid declined to leave, and he was then forcibly ejected.' Since 1918, when Stonehenge became the property of the nation, the Druids have suffered no comparable harassment.

Above: The Pontypridd Rocking Stone in South Wales, which has long been the scene of oratory and ceremonial by Welsh Druids and revivalists. In his unsuccessful General Election campaign of 1910 the Labour candidate, Mr G.B. Stanton, followed tradition by holding a meeting at the Rocking Stone.

Right: Tynwald Hill, the seat of the Manx parliament, was a Norse Thing, or mound of democratic assembly, and before that a prehistoric, possibly Neolithic site. It is said to be built up of soil from each of the parishes in the Isle of Man. The 1962 photograph shows the annual reading of the laws, and the eighteenth-century watercolour of the same site is by Godfrey.

Left: An assembly of Cornish Bards at the Boscawen-un stone circle, traditionally one of the chief Gorsedd centres, or bardic meeting places, in Britain. The Cornish Bards, reconstituted in 1928, borrowed most of their ceremonial from the Welsh Druids, but they are distinguished by their sky-blue robes.

Left and opposite: Three examples of faith in the magical powers of certain rocks. The first (*left*) is one of the curious signals found near the junction of the Yellowstone and Missouri Rivers by Prince Maximilian zu Wied (1841). They were designed by the Indians 'for the purpose of attracting the bison herds, and to have a successful hunt'. The Stone Mare rock of Locronon and the Christianized menhir by a village church, both in Brittany (*opposite*), are the customary resorts of women seeking to bear children.

Below: Photographic study of a summer landscape, made early this century, with the Wiltshire landmark, the Devil's Den near Avebury.

Three obvious examples of churches which were sited on or near native shrines: the church and tall menhir at Rudston, Yorkshire; Knowlton church, Dorset, built within the earthworks of an ancient henge monument; the church of St Columba, Glencolumbkille, County Donegal. The great stone in the foreground at Glencolumbkille, one of several which formerly stood about the church, now marks a station on the annual pilgrimage which takes place on St Columba's feast day, 15 June. He is said to have expelled a host of demons from the site.

List of illustrations

Index